WORKING THROUGH

Other books by Leonard Kriegel

THE LONG WALK HOME

THE ESSENTIAL WORKS OF THE FOUNDING FATHERS

EDMUND WILSON

WORKING THROUGH

A Teacher's Journey in the Urban University

LEONARD KRIEGEL

Saturday Review Press · New York

Library of Congress Catalog Card Number: 72-79054

ISBN 0-8415-0186-6

Saturday Review Press
230 Park Avenue
New York, New York 10017

PRINTED IN THE UNITED STATES OF AMERICA

Design by Tere LoPrete

FOR MINA SHAUGHNESSY,
who knows that nothing is learned simply

Preface

This book constitutes a personal and selective record of academic experience. It was written because so much recent writing about higher education in America lacks the felt experience, the way things actually are. In certain respects, the problems of being either a student or a teacher in the United States today have become more abstract even as they have been made more public. Higher education is probably now under more intense scrutiny than any other aspect of American institutional life. Books, newspapers, periodicals, all are filled with advice, much of it gratuitous, much of it well-intentioned, for our colleges and universities. The ills which afflict the American academic world are outnumbered only by the panaceas offered to cure those ills.

I do not claim to have the answers to "the crisis in

higher education." I am no longer convinced that there are any answers. We will simply have to struggle with our problems and find our own way of dealing with them. I have tried to depict that struggle and explain how it affected me personally as a student and a professor in the urban university.

I find that I have written a book which portrays my own experience in the academic world as "representative" despite my strong belief in the uniqueness of each man's experience. As an undergraduate, I learned that I had to establish the boundaries of my own confusion by myself; as a teacher, I learned that I had to accept the confusion of my students. There are no substitutes for the self.

Between 1951 and 1960, I attended three different colleges or universities as a student. Since 1960 I have been a full-time member of the college teaching profession. The institutions at which I have studied and taught range from a prestigious Ivy League school to an urban university that is poorly endowed and faced with an uncertain future. The schools share only function and geography: they are all academic institutions located in New York City. But their problems as well as their prospects are shared by other urban colleges and universities. Each of them forms part of the educational spectrum available to urban students. New York is not as singular as either its critics or its public relations men believe; it is merely a larger urban center than most. I am convinced that the academic world forms a significant part of the urban world as it currently exists. If we can use the university as a prototype, it may yet prove to be a source of man's salvation in his cities.

WORKING THROUGH

Chapter One

I am, purely by accident, a man representative of a certain time and a certain set of experiences. Born in the thirties, I am a child of the fifties, though I am not part of what has come to be called middle America. Nor was I endowed with the belief that this is the American century, that I could claim its legacy as my own because I was as natural an heir as anyone else. But I inherited the century's liabilities and they shaped the coming of age of my generation of college teachers. To most of us who lived through the decade as students, the fifties suggest a lack of outline and definition, a sense of potential tragedy but no players willing to suffer in their designated roles. "I saw the best minds of my generation destroyed by madness," writes Allen Ginsberg in the opening line of *Howl*. The catalog he evokes is of a suffering without real focus, a country of the mind so immense that it threatens to take away even the capacity to suffer. Ginsberg caught us not so much as we were but as we desired to be portrayed: spiritually starved, mentally beaten, our intellects somehow mangled, our souls atrophied. This is our memory of our own coming of age. And yet, much as we once felt obligated to depict our lives, our educations, even our marriages as both quiescent and despairing, we now object that we have been too eagerly believed. Before *Howl*, there was Mr. Eliot's *Prufrock*. Any number of professors told us J. Alfred was ours by right of legacy. He, too, is afraid of being too eagerly believed. "That is not what I meant at all," he cries to an indifferent world. Our generation has already been delivered to history for judgment. We were *silent*, a chilling word in the accusation it rouses up. The indictment is total; it offers no way out. We failed even as witnesses, for we did not speak up when we should have.

The indictment is undoubtedly honest but a bit too presumptuous. My generation had its doubts and struggles, but not all of them can be attributed to cowardice. The world that we had inherited as adolescents in August, 1945, had begun to disintegrate even before we could see the necessity of setting it right. By 1950, the year before I entered college, not one of us could be overly optimistic about our possibilities of getting through to the sixties. It was evident that more than intelligence was needed; we needed luck. Since there did not seem to be very much of that around on the international scene, we turned into ourselves for the necessary decisions and choices. While the smiling general was groomed for the White House and the man whom we had, as

4

schoolchildren, affectionately called Uncle Joe spun the barrel in his own version of Russian roulette, we were forced to recognize that the choices were limited. Our chief concern was whether or not World War III would follow World War II. Everything else was beside the point.

I was born a few months after Franklin Delano Roosevelt wheeled his patrician confidence into the White House to tell my parents, European Jewish immigrants, that they had nothing to fear but fear itself. One of my earliest memories of formal education is walking the corridors of P.S. 80 in the Bronx thinking about the previous evening's news, Gabriel Heatter's intimately somber accents reciting the tonnage and number of American ships sunk. Ultimately, however, the ships got through, Hitler's Germany surrendered, we dropped an atom bomb on Japan, and pictures of the rubble of Hiroshima and the mounds of arms and legs that formed the landscape of the Nazi death camps collided in our minds. The war was over. The heroic age should have begun anew then, and yet I don't think that any of us believed that it would. Those newsreels with the mounds of bodies and the image of the mushrooming cloud lingered in one's memory. The future was fragile.

It is difficult to unscramble the memories. The late forties were fast-moving years. The events fuse and lock into one another to form a total picture: the second Louis-Conn fight; survivors of Auschwitz peering through barbed wire fences on Cyprus; the Berlin airlift, which I would have settled simply by doing away with Berlin. At fifteen, I considered myself a socialist, but socialism simply represented the way in which I would prefer the messiah to arrive. Since I did not really expect the messiah, I held on to socialism as my Italian friends held on to Catholicism—not as a firm credo but as an indefinite goal.

September, 1951, was a peculiar time to enter college. The very insanity of our potential fate made us narrow our focus. Although we remained aware of what was happening outside the college gates, we wanted to solidify the foothold our parents and grandparents had gained in this country. Certainly, we believed in the goals and aims of society more than students today; we had less cause to mistrust those goals. The sense of impending doom began to fade after both the United States and the Soviet Union exploded hydrogen bombs, and we simply began to adjust ourselves to the fact that politically there was no real place to stand. Socialism had thrown off a great deal of its vitality when it rid itself of the lies and distortions of Soviet history. It was easier to say, "A plague on both your houses," ignore politics, and concentrate on our own affairs. We found ourselves in love with this country for what it could be and turning away from it because of what it was. What member of my generation has not read the final pages of Mailer's *The Armies of the Night* without an embarrassed smile of recognition? For it was we, the children of the Left, who were wooing the lady now; Mailer was writing about our own "dream of love." This was our country making the distinctions for the world. The bomb was ours, the senator from Wisconsin was ours, the Cold War was ours, Korea was ours. Our friends, our relatives, ultimately we ourselves (unless, of course, one escaped with a 4F) were pulled into the army.

This was simply the natural order of things. The Korean War stirred no hearts, but it stirred no protest

6

either. Stalinism had compromised the Left virtually out of existence; liberalism seemed a dead end, lifeless and lacking in vision and incredibly defensive; conservatism could be no more than a minor whim. We heard no voices forceful enough to sway us to one side or the other, and so we seemed to stand between two worlds. On one side was the swell of populism and liberalism that had jelled into the New Deal and the legacy, however incomplete, that it left the country. On the other, a mood that was wary of change and had turned in upon itself. It had convinced us that we were tired; we actually shared with the Soviets the conviction that systems alone were now needed in the affairs of men, for systems could stand independent of ideology and perhaps even of man himself. It was this belief that Eisenhower reflected so successfully—not in what he said or what his advisers told him but in the bland geniality of his face and smile. Although I distrusted what he stood for, I had to admit that he had caught the public's hand and that he was holding it with the assurance of a suitor who knows that in his eyes alone hovers the image of his beloved. He made us a bit more confident of our immediate survival. Having no possibility that promised to justify an alternative risk, we went to school, worked for grades, sought to become a part of American society.

I suppose an argument can be made that I am not representative. Between the end of my fifth-grade year and the morning in September, 1951, when I walked into a 9 A.M. section of freshman English, I was never in a "normal" classroom situation. I spent the years between 1944 and 1946 in a hospital trying to combat the effects of polio. I did my last year of grade school and my four years of high school on home instruction. But if this sets me apart, it does not weaken my claim. In fact, it enforces it, since during those sequestering years I had retained an educational innocence my friends had had to abandon in order to survive in New York City's high schools. When I entered college, I was far hungrier for education than they; I was both more expectant and less skeptical of the college experience. I very much wanted to learn, to read whatever was worth reading. It was obvious to me that I knew very little. I was fortunate since, having survived as a cripple, I suspect that I possessed a stronger sense of self and perhaps a better-developed sense of competitiveness than most of my fellow students. I probably had read more than most of them, too. To a cripple, time seems inescapable and reading is a way in which to make time yield itself. Yet I was ignorant of things my friends accepted without question. I had never set foot in a high school science laboratory, never peered through a microscope, never participated in a student election. Even the drawings of an amoeba that I made were crudely copied out of a biology textbook.

I had no war against the system. Despite my nominal socialism, I was willing to accept society at its own value, and if this was not the best of all possible worlds, it remained the one in which I was living. Whatever rebellion existed within me was strictly personal, involving ways to avoid the traps that society sets for the cripple. When I entered Hunter, my friends were the sons and daughters of garment cutters, fur dressers, electricians, taxi drivers, and bartenders. We shared certain assumptions about the world, and we hesitated before making demands upon it. There were still expectations of success, but we were not altogether convinced that the kind of success illustrated inside the covers of *Life* magazine was what we wanted. All we assumed about success was that it would enable us to lead a different life than our parents had lived. Whether life would prove to be more exciting remained to be seen.

Had I not been crippled, I suppose I would have ended up at the City College of New York, where I now teach. This was the destination most of us accepted as our own. Few of my friends had parents who could afford to pay tuition. City was *the* municipal college. Brooklyn College and Queens College were both distant and unreal. Until the announcement that Hunter College in the Bronx would take male students in the September, 1951, entering class, this school had accepted only girls, who went there for two years before transferring to the Park Avenue branch.

I chose to attend Hunter simply because City demanded a longer and more difficult subway ride. I was somewhat dubious about a school that was changing over from an all-girls to a coeducational institution. (City had also changed from an all-boys to a coeducational institution that year.) It made no difference, however. I was so eager to attend a real school once again and to sit in a classroom that I would have gone to Hunter even if it had actually been the convent that my City-bound friends claimed it was.

Physically, it was pleasing enough. It possessed stretches of grassy lawns, a relatively inoffensive W.P.A. imitation-Gothic architecture, and an elaborate labyrinth of underground tunnels that provided shelter on fierce winter days. There were incongruities in the appearance of the campus, but they enforced the impression that the college was not quite what it seemed to be. The nation had become defense-oriented, and along with the entrance of our class the army erected a radar battery, accompanied by three or four anti-aircraft guns, on the weed-strewn lots that hugged the small reservoir across the street from the college. If the politics of conspiracy had any basis in reality, Hunter should have been among the safer spots in America. There were still people in the neighborhoods surrounding it whose view of the world was created by *The Daily Worker*, although by 1951 they carefully folded it inside the larger *New York Times*. Yet the guns seemed merely decorative and the quonset huts housed lonely boys from Arkansas who whistled at the girl students legging their way from Gillette Hall to Davis Hall. It was all very American.

I preferred the other side of the campus, though, which offered the exposed tracks of the Independent Line's subway depot and the sound of rattling trains, empty and liberated from their run. Their tired clanking distantly echoed through our classrooms as a reminder of a world we all were determined to leave; it seemed the ritual gasping of industrial civilization. I would occasionally walk over to the depot and stand and watch the trains roll in and out and find myself caught up in the rhythms and conversation of men and their machines. At that time, most of the transit workers were still Irish, and I would sometimes encounter a few old-line anarchists who had never been convinced that Cardinal Spellman was the truest friend the working man ever had. Even their sons, they would grudgingly admit, were attending Fordham and St. Francis and spoke of careers as stockbrokers or advertising executives as they scanned the help-wanted columns in the *Times*. "Can you imagine, now," one of them groaned during his lunch hour as he chewed away at a huge ham and cheese sandwich, "the little bastard thinks the *Post* is a goddam radical paper? *Radical* he calls it. Can you imagine?"

Just above the college were a series of baseball fields and athletic grounds that disintegrated into the looming spire of De Witt Clinton High School. Clinton, once an excellent school, was steadily losing ground to the prestigious Bronx High School of Science. A few years after my graduation, Science built its new quarters between Hunter and Clinton, intended no doubt as a symbol of aspiration for one, of reality for the other. Below our campus was the all-girls Walton High School. Both Walton and Clinton now send graduates to Hunter. In New York's educational world, provincialism was fed by geography.

The most humiliating experience of my first academic year took place on the day I registered. Registration is the first of many endurance tests a college student must face before he is certified as ready to leave. I remember the experience as exhausting, a cacophonous blend of shrill-voiced teachers peddling courses and class sections and the swell of voices in a cafeteria filled with nervous, confused men and gum-chewing, sweat-stained young women, all verging on hysteria. The chief problem that the entering student faced, aside from simply making physical progress on whichever line he found himself, was to authenticate the rumors that were floating around. Who was the professor said to make his freshman class memorize the entire first chapter of the *Iliad*? What was freshman orientation? If you arrived with three years of high school French, exactly what sequence of French courses were you expected to follow? What was the name of the psychology professor who cared so little about grades that he would change them merely upon request?

A male teacher was standing on top of a wooden cafeteria table shouting, "No one can consider himself a college student unless he has at least one eighth-hour class." The image of academic dignity shriveled and died. I jammed myself against the wall, holding on to my crutches as if they were clubs that I might need for self-defense. I searched the mimeographed lists of numbers and letters that designated courses offered, courses withdrawn, courses open, courses required, obligations, oaths, tests of citizenship, promises not to overthrow the country or the cafeteria tables, pledges of good intentions, the right to breathe in the heady groves of academe.

I can easily fathom the rage of many students today against the educational system. They see it as a visible embodiment of all that is wrong with America. My own initiation to the bureaucracy of academia is testimony to their arguments. It could not simply be dismissed as poor bureaucratic functioning; the rage I felt was simply too personal to grant that. I would certainly argue the legitimacy of fighting against an inept bureaucracy without demanding the overthrow of an entire political and economic system, but the truth is that what I felt during those hours at registration was a rising desire to get even, to force *them* to endure what my peers and I were being forced to endure. Registration should have been a minor event in my college career; instead, I emerged from it feeling that I had been stripped of some integral aspect of myself. Indeed, the first lesson in my college education was that my sense of self meant nothing to the college bureaucracy. It was probably less shocking to my fellow students, who had simply exchanged the red tape of a municipal high school for the red tape of a municipal college. On this first infuriating day, I felt unsure that I could even function, let alone bring my ideas into focus, in a world so willing to ignore my presence. We had been paired off, the municipal educational system and I. We were to be enemies, and the first round belonged to the system. I finally took whatever they were willing to give me, approaching each table as a humble supplicant. Nothing mattered except to get out. Once I made that decision, however, I found myself with the very program I had wanted. I handed my completed program and course cards to a lady who was the final hurdle before my exit at the check-out counter.

"You're a lucky young man," she said.

"Why?"

"Just look behind you." I turned around to see swarms of students still hustling from table to table. One girl was alternately laughing and crying in front of a table marked "Physical Education" behind which an adamant woman defensively sat. Another girl was quietly sobbing in a corner. "You're certainly lucky to have finished so early."

"It's just God's blessing, lady," I said. She looked at me sharply, and I quickly apologized. I had visions of being forced to return to all those lines. The battle was drawn, my real education could begin. I didn't want to shop around anymore. Anyway, I was too tired to think of resistance.

My first year in college helped to convince me that, while the times were dangerous, they were not yet uncontrollable. I still had choices. I could study for pleasure, and I could study in order to prepare myself to live. Doctor, lawyer, Indian chief, it didn't matter. The fact that Hunter, like City and Brooklyn and Queens, was a subway college meant that I would not have to give it the luxury of permanence. For the next four years it was the center of my life. But it was a center with no anchor of its own. It led me to the Village, to the Metropolitan Museum of Art, to the Lower East Side. It never constricted me, and in some ways it served me generously. A movable center evokes no sense of loss.

Like most American colleges, it had experienced a boom with the arrival of veterans going to school on the G.I. bill after the war. The school's admission of veterans had been deemed a temporary measure. By the time I arrived, the World War II veterans were virtually gone, while the Korean War veterans had not yet arrived. The year 1951 brought men into the college as a permanent measure. A year or two after I left, the student population of Hunter College in the Bronx numbered more men than women, a change that was ultimately to lead to its independence from the Park Avenue branch of the school. When I attended the college, I was one of 225 men surrounded by 2,000 women.

The male students in this first co-ed class were in one way or another misfits in municipal college education. Their high school averages were a point or two lower than those of students applying to City. I suspect that they were both more neurotic and more conventional than City's students. Unlike the students I was later to confront at Columbia, nobody at Hunter was particularly interested in slashing his way through your soul, not even with an intellectual razor. The students were skeptical, but skeptical about themselves rather than about the outside world or the college. If they could have voiced their deepest educational aspirations, their cry would have been "Make me a person!" rather than "Educate me!" There was a prevalent idea that education was supposed to mold you, although none of us was sure what the ideal form should be.

Most male students in the class of '55 came from working-class or lower-middle-class backgrounds, most were Jewish, and most were from the Bronx. The girls in our class offered a more varied ethnic and class background. A number were comfortable middle class, the daughters of doctors, small businessmen, or lawyers. Had the girls been boys, they would have been sent out of town, for their futures would then have been at stake. Even for those who could afford it, spending money on the education of a woman when a "free" college was available was a dubious proposition.

Despite coeducation, Hunter had maintained its reputation as the Catholic college among the four municipal colleges. The president of the school was a distinguished Catholic scholar, and the school administration was rumored to be as much the product of Democratic party politics as it was of educational achievement. Unlike City and Brooklyn, Hunter uptown was "safe," untinged by a radical past.

The faculty on the Bronx campus was fairly interesting. There were not many academic achievers, but rather professors who felt uncomfortable with the approaching changes in academic life. During the fifties, the American university was assuming greater and greater importance, yet most of my teachers at Hunter did not perceive the growing power and influence of education in postwar American life. A majority did not approve of the college's going coeducational, for they assumed that their own lives would be less tranquil after this happened.

In the past, Hunter had possessed a reputation as an outstanding women's college, the only public institution that could be mentioned alongside Vassar and Radcliffe and other excellent women's colleges. The reputation was deserved, for the school had provided its graduates with as demanding an education as any school in the country. Once the decision to make City College co-educational had been made, however, Hunter inevitably followed in City's steps. The brighter and more aggressive women headed toward Convent Avenue. For some members of the faculty, especially for several dedicated women who firmly believed in what they had been doing, the new arrangement proved to be unsatisfactory. Most of the male students who entered Hunter in 1951 were intellectually inferior to the women who had attended since the thirties. It was even more difficult for the faculty to accept the fact that Hunter was no longer attracting the brightest of New York City's female high school graduates. "It wasn't that the girls that we used to have were brighter," said a professor in the German department to me. "I suspect that they were. Still, that wasn't as important as the fact that they were serious. They were interested in ideas. Your class seemed so frivolous; maybe that's because it was the first coeducational class. The veterans, of course, were different. They had no time for nonsense. The girls—that's what really depresses me. Hunter girls used to be so exciting to teach. But those girls you were with, they seemed so tired, so dead. Not many of them cared for anything, not even for the men."

It was certainly true that the vast majority of my peers were not particularly oriented toward intellectual discipline. In one respect, the class of '55 was fortunate. There was far less pressure to succeed than there had been for Hunter classes in the past. The pressure that once had been welcomed at Hunter had been dissipated through the years. Even the Korean War veterans who began to arrive during my second year at Hunter did not bring with them a desire to achieve. They changed neither the school nor the student body, and as a group they were dedicated to the same idea of college life as we were. Somewhere along the road, whether in the service or before, they had been impressed by the fact that you could earn more with a college degree than with a high school diploma. College was economically desirable. But this was different from the academic pressures of the post-Sputnik era, when Americans were systematically sold the idea that the nation's colleges and universities were the backbone of democracy, the cradle of liberty, the source of all potency. Americans were to be taught, in fact, that the nation's ability to make love, war, peace, and children ultimately depended upon what educators throughout the land had begun to call "our human resources."

The fact that Hunter was not an academic pressure cooker was a distinct advantage for some of us. A student could be educated to the extent that he wished to be. Or else he could choose, as the majority of students did choose, not to think about the world or about what he wanted from an education. Here were courses that seemed mere exercises in hagiography: literature courses in which the sole emphasis was upon the biographical minutiae that plague the lives of writers as they plague the lives of all men. Some of my teachers taught as if they had never heard of textual explication.

Today the study of literature seems to suffer from a

desperate quest for modernity and fashionability, and so courses spread uncontrollably over a virtually unlimited range. My own education, however, suffered from a lingering sense of constriction that frequently made me think of literature as a hothouse plant. The best English teacher I had once proudly boasted to me that he had never read Dostoevsky or those whom he disdainfully referred to as "the Russians" (by whom he meant not Mayakovsky but Tolstoy and Turgenev). "Shakespeare and the Elizabethans are good enough for me." The professor was an anachronism. Not even time would challenge so entrenched a view of literature and the world. Modern literature was simply a historical mistake as far as he was concerned.

And yet, however parochial his temperament, he offered me a point of view against which I had to challenge my own conception of what was and was not important. I admired him, and I owed a great deal to him. He did revere his discipline even if he granted it only the vitality of scholarship. He never pretended that the study of literature was intended as the channel to levers of power; he never pretended that it was supposed to *do* anything for the student other than to reward his curiosity and intelligence and to satisfy his aesthetic needs. He did not have to worry about being relevant; it was enough that he loved Shakespeare, that he taught his subject well enough so that I began to study the texts myself, that he was able to make me feel that a scholarly response could also be a genuine response, and that he permitted me to make my own connections with the material. He was my teacher, not my nurse. And the role of teacher suited him. By the time I had begun to think seriously of going on to graduate school and becoming a teacher of

18

English, I had to ask myself exactly what my own obligations were going to be when it came to the teaching of literature. It is a question I still have not answered to my own satisfaction. I doubt that I ever will. But it seems to me that, were I forced to choose between what he gave to me as a teacher and what many of my contemporaries give to their students, my choice would be what I had taken from him.

At the same time, my education suffered from an inability to entertain the very paradoxes and problems that produce real intellectual vitality. Ideas were subordinate to facts, to given realities. Hunter was not altogether at home with the mind. The political scientist who had served in the state assembly was determined to demonstrate *how* government worked to his freshmen and sophomores, but he ignored the question of what it worked for, just as he ignored the question of who benefited from its working. I had been dipping into Marx at that time. My professor was wary of an interest even as casual as mine was, though not because of the political threat of the times. Marx simply offended his need for the practical.

"Look," he explained kindly, after I had asked him a question about the origins of Marxism, "you really ought to avoid that kind of thinking. It just doesn't do very much for you in this class."

"Why not?"

"Because it's useless. It simply has nothing to do with the actual way, the *real* way, in which societies are governed. Don't misunderstand me. I'm not questioning your right to ask such questions. Theories simply take away from the real problems of government. They're a waste of time. It's a luxury that no true politician can afford. And a political scientist should never permit himself the kind of luxury not open to men in government. It's absolutely senseless. Political science is a tool. And a tool only helps insofar as it's useful. That's the Marxist problem in this country. In all countries. Nothing could be further removed from the realities of the way government actually works than Marxism."

This was the way in which government was taught in the fifties. The pragmatic, the practical, was instinctively justified. Government was stripped of any ideological or even spiritual proportions it might have possessed and was presented in terms of performance alone. The student was offered the opportunity to study a system whose chief virtue was that it functioned.

Hunter had become part of Eisenhower's America. There was no ivory tower here either. Even in 1951, American education was self-consciously part of what cab drivers and stockbrokers alike called "the real world." Its concerns were overwhelmingly with that world, and the job of the university was to prepare each of us for our roles. Even the study of literature had to be justified. The irony was that my peers and I could have used a certain distance from the world then, a place from which to measure what was happening to us. A little irrelevance, I was eventually to discover, could be an asset for the soul struggling with its own secrets.

I was under few illusions about Hunter when I was a student. I did spend four comparatively happy and enlightening years there, however, and I was taught by a number of people who were content to educate me without feeling obliged to remold me in their own image. There was a very clear understanding between students and faculty. We did not tread on one another's territory. None of my instructors wanted to interfere with the Jewish working-class milieu out of which I came; they never urged me to throw it away like an old suit of clothes, nor did they expect me to parade it like some exotic neckerchief.

The distance that existed between me and my teachers served me well. It enabled me to define my own individuality, to claim a degree of self-respect and, at the same time, to choose from among a variety of intellectual pursuits. Despite today's talk about the need for personal relationships between teacher and student, despite the voices angrily declaiming against being mere ciphers on omnipresent I.B.M. cards, I sometimes wonder whether it is not the student's very individuality that is being distorted by teachers too intent on being his friend. I would never have asked my teachers for personal advice. That was not their function. And I was not interested in being their friend. We were both interested in books, but we did not use that interest to inflict our egos upon each other. Natural boundaries were natural boundaries, and we both recognized and respected that fact. Today, however, the line between teacher and student is supposed to disappear. Insofar as this allows for intellectual equality it is all to the good. However, if it is designed to make the university into a social club, then it serves only to diminish a university's true function. And I prefer the arrangement I had with my teachers.

Most of them considered their profession to have distinctly limited goals. Good or bad, intellectual or nonintellectual, I can remember few whose lives were so anchored to Hunter College that college teaching became a substitute for other kinds of experience. Looking back, I am impressed that they never encouraged their students to emulate them. However minor, even trivial, this may seem, it impresses me because so many of us today react to the world as if we were engaged in some psychic crap game run by literalists of the imagination. We are the very people who want intellect to do something positive, to re-create the world so that passion for the image is all, to sacrifice the private self to the public symbol in the name of art or science. We are more interested in timeliness than in truth. The individual consciousness of the student must eventually decide whether or not Shakespeare is timely. The kind of educational hucksterism that seeks to placate young minds with the placebos of contemporaneity simply cannot do it. When I first read Tolstoy for a class in comparative literature, I was not particularly aware of whether or not his ethics would change my life. I worked that out for myself in my own good time.

I did not know why men studied literature or why they studied sociology or why, for that matter, they studied anything that could not be immediately translated into one or another profession. I did know that the study of literature made intellectual sense to me. To the credit of my undergraduate teachers, they nurtured this interest, in large part by permitting it to satisfy itself.

Nor am I quite sure of why history still appealed to us. For whatever reason, it was a crucible in which both literature and we ourselves had been formed. Our students today are ahistorical; this seems to me established beyond argument. They deal with the past by ignoring its existence. None of the explanations I have heard for this reaction are satisfactory, although McLuhan is probably closest to the mark when he singles out the technological changes in our society since World War II. Somehow I assume that this would make literature more rather than less central. Humanistic education enabled one to resist the drift into technological stasis, a drift that one could see everywhere. Literature became meaningful for me because it dealt in realities that were strictly personal. I believe that this should hold true for students today, but I have to admit that both their response and their relationship to literature, like their response and relationship to ideas, seem terribly impersonal; I am more skeptical about whether this represents a "new consciousness."

Perhaps the insistence on relevance will bring a millennium in its wake. The question can only be answered in the future. But one reads literature with an expectation that it will communicate, that it is important to pull out of literature something more than an idealistic vision. You keep it personal and immediate in order to keep it.

At Hunter, literature was given no special place of its own. I took the traditional four-year liberal arts curriculum, which included a large number of required courses in several disciplines, a required major subject of twenty-four credits and a minor subject of twelve credits. It was an intellectual potpourri, and it left much to be desired. There were all sorts of packages, something for everybody. It did succeed, however, in making me aware of a great deal that I had not been aware of earlier. During the past decade, the traditional liberal arts curriculum has been attacked so often that its survival today is highly questionable. It is obvious that teachers no longer feel certain that it deserves to survive. And yet one must speak of its virtues as well as its failings. There was so much I needed to know, so much I had to be introduced to when I was in college. Perhaps we are guilty of assuming in our students today a sophistication and a complacency that they do not possess. They have acquired a kind of preprocessed political packaging, like slices of cheese wrapped in clear plastic. Slogans may not be history, but we have a great deal of difficulty in convincing our students of that.

Inevitably the range of teaching at Hunter reflected a variety not only of talent but of experience. Although the professor of government endowed the discipline with a peculiarly drab pragmatism, I encountered a young sociology instructor who made the behavior of men more understandable as he traced certain outlines in Western social and political thought. A teacher's voice could trill without understanding when she mentioned the name Emerson. In another class, the teacher whose job it was to introduce us to psychology spent most of his time telling us about the problems of writing for the *Saturday Evening Post* and living in Scarsdale. But there were others, too. I was taught philosophy by a man with whom I ultimately did an independent study tutorial, whose brilliantly analytical intelligence forced me to defend all my intellectual positions.

The courses I took in my first years of college appealed to me, perhaps because I was unsophisticated. For me, they did what they were supposed to do. They introduced me to a variety of subjects about which I was astoundingly ignorant. The established curriculum led me into a wider intellectual world than the one I had known and let me choose for myself what I wished to take and what I felt I could just as well leave alone. I suppose it is highly debatable whether greater consciousness of science and art is desirable. I do not know if I am any *happier* than an Australian aborigine. I know, though, that I wanted a wider world and I was grateful that it was offered to me.

Education is usually thought of as a heightening of consciousness and the creation of greater intellectual awareness. This happened to me at Hunter. I remember a one-credit course required of all students, an introduction to art history. I cannot conceive of conditions less conducive to teaching. The sessions I attended had more than a hundred students, some of whom simply slept their way through the term's work when the lights went off and the slides began to project against the screen. Like so many other young teachers at Hunter, the instructor was in the process of completing his Ph.D. in art history. He chain-smoked cigarettes, gazing nervously above us as he spoke, a man given to ticlike spasms of energy that made him appear physically isolated on the auditorium stage, as if somewhere within those slides lurked the potential escape for him, too, a long tunnel carved through the circles of whatever it was that had brought him to the study of art. He was a magnificent teacher. He managed to create the beginnings of a consciousness of art in me, as form and as history. Perhaps it would have been created anyway. Yet it was his course, as far as I am concerned, that forced me into one more encounter with the world of art and intellect. He sent me scurrying to the Metropolitan Museum of Art, a not-inconsiderable achievement. I had been ready for the study of literature simply by having been an avid reader, but I was deeply suspicious of the world of museums and of a kind of culture still dominated by money and class. Art was much more threatening than literature since it posed a challenge to my own narrow territory of the spirit. His lectures made art terribly vital, imaginatively alive. The man was dedicated to his subject, not to his students. But that didn't matter. If anything, it worked to my advantage. I didn't need him. I needed what he was teaching.

I took that class during a period in which American academic life was threatened by fierce political repression. And yet, I cannot claim that I really remember ever having been conscious of that threat in the classroom. One of the paradoxes of my recollections is that the college seemed relatively free as far as expression goes. Obviously it wasn't. Two or three professors had already been threatened with dismissal by the time I arrived. The municipal college system, like the nation at large, was intent on purifying itself. During my second year, three professors teaching at the downtown branch of the college were forced to resign. The school's president denounced the Communist affiliations of one of the student political clubs, then pleaded for academic freedom, no doubt aware that, as a prominent Catholic layman and the former allied high commissioner for Bavaria, he possessed relative immunity from the hysteria whipped up by Joseph McCarthy. But on the uptown campus, politics was a tame enough affair. I certainly met no one intent on bringing down the country.

With one or two strictly vocal exceptions, I cannot remember anyone to the left of Adlai Stevenson. It even caused a slight furor when the school newspaper endorsed Stevenson for president in 1952. A discreet note entered all political conversations, even those between student and student, a kind of voluntary self-censorship. Caution was not exactly our watchword, but we were faithful to the mood of the country. We tended to ignore the reality and the threat of intellectual repression. I suppose that the students simply emulated the faculty. The way in which American universities and colleges capitulated before the onslaught of the senator from Wisconsin and his legions is sufficiently well known to need no repeating here. No single episode has filled the academic community with greater or more deserved shame.

My education was not intended to make me politically critical; it was designed to make me cautious, to make me choose judiciously between alternatives that were, in the words of my instructor in political science, "real enough for consideration." At the same time, the kind of political pressure that was exerted never touched me directly. Books were neither barred nor burned, manners remained in style, and a certain note of propriety was struck both by educators and by editorial writers for the *Times*. I suppose that I was all too willing to give up politics for the time being. Still I cannot help but note that my generation felt that it was not altogether constricted, that there were choices available so that individuals could decide how they would function within the society. Such choices seemed genuine enough at the time. Perhaps it was, at least in my own case, the fact that we were very much like our parents, still tied to the idea of a nation of immigrants. I looked on my education very much as my parents did. They assumed that an "educated man" (a phrase they used quite frequently) lived better not because he had more (although that was undoubtedly a part of it) but because education was the kind of resource that enabled one to control the way in which he lived. An educated man possessed style, and nothing offered greater appeal to the sons and daughters of the working and lower-middle classes. Money was necessary in order to escape from traps; style was necessary so that one could make choices. I never considered my education as the route to economic security, although I knew that I wanted to earn enough money to live better than my father had. I wonder now whether money was as central to us as we have been told, whether our choices of professions and jobs were really dictated by economics. When, for example, I abandoned the notion of becoming a lawyer in order to become a teacher, it was not because I considered the profession as the route to success, nor was it out of a desire for security. Law simply seemed inadequate, a justification of its own acquisitiveness, while teaching seemed to demand a certain sense of dedication. So many people I knew in college made similar choices: from pre-law to the foreign service, from medicine to the rabbinate, from teaching to designing jewelry. I was, like many other students in that most materialistic of times, committed to a future that would please me rather than one that would make me wealthy.

Education at Hunter bred in me a need to be useful, a service mentality that remains something I still find myself fighting as a teacher. We were, after all, the last generation in America to accept the idea that work was something that we had to perform simply to stay alive. We wanted interesting careers, but we always remembered the depression, vaguely from our own experiences, but vividly from our parents' stories. The problem facing us was to be whatever we wanted to be but to make enough money so that we could exist in comfort. I accepted without resistance the premise that my education was intended to send me into the American marketplace. My generation revered the pragmatic and distrusted ideology, primarily because we believed that ideology victimized men. This proved to be another of our errors in judgment. And yet, and this is where we possessed a distinct advantage over many more politically minded students today, it would not have occurred to us that an attitude could be substituted for an ideology.

Education in the fifties depended finally upon one's own attitudes. In a sense, the student created his own relevance because he never expected the teacher to create it for him. Relevance was not to be achieved at the expense of a general paralysis of intelligence. Any education was bound to fail or, at best, to be only partially successful. This hard fact seemed to me then, as it still seems to me today, one more aspect of the nature of reality. The world's complexity would remain despite the education I received at Hunter or anywhere else. Whatever sense I made out of the chaotic impressions I received, both within and without the classroom, would represent an imposition of my point of view upon the world. My responsibility was fairly limited: to learn as much as possible and to define a point of view for myself. My teachers could assume a certain intelligence on my part; I, in turn, could assume a certain good will on theirs. If I proved to be capable of taking what they had to offer, fine; if not, there would be others whom they could teach.

No one needed to convince me that learning could be fun; no one, to my knowledge, ever attempted to motivate me. I feel strangely grateful for these negative gifts today. For it permitted me distance, and distance provided me with a sense of discovery. Despite its very obvious shortcomings, its parochialism, its fear of the contemporary, its lingering touch of a girl's finishing school, the undergraduate education I received at Hunter seems to me, at this distance, not to have been a waste. My college education provided me with certain barriers to the cultural explosion we are experiencing today. My professors believed in what they taught. I was forced to confront a world that was strange and appealing by a Catholic Aristotelean who taught me philosophy. I had to struggle with a certain intellectual perspective in order to resist its attractiveness and order. I read modern literature in the face of a faculty openly hostile to the modern and openly contemptuous of anything produced in America (a breadbasket and nothing more, was the implication, to which barbarism clung like barnacles). This forced me to think about what I believed a culture might achieve, to root out issues as well as answers for myself rather than to discover that both issues and answers had been formulated by one or another abstraction. My teachers presented their views as a challenge; the response was left up to me. I doubt whether they were particularly conscious of what they were doing, yet I am glad they did it. My reaction to them today leads me to suspect that a bit of spiritual and intellectual distance can be benign. They were interested in me and in my future, yet they remained more interested in their disciplines. In that lay the source of whatever power they could claim.

Whenever I drift back to my undergraduate days, I soon pass by the school's neo-Gothic architecture, the frequently parochial administration, even the faculty that served me well, to call the roll of my friends there. I think of the suicide of Stephanie, of how even at Hunter she spent her time trying to be the daughter her parents wanted. The note she left behind in the bathroom of a dilapidated West Side hotel begged her mother's forgiveness. Not having been the daughter she was expected to be, she had taken her revenge. Hunter never taught her very much in the way of resistance. I think of Owen, dead in his early thirties, who introduced me to Dos Passos' *USA*, who was virginal and shy and who conceived of literature as an entrée into the world of high society. He wanted to be a writer so that he could eat at Sardi's and become a "personality." To be recognized, known, identified as a picture in the papers. He died, too, about a year after his play, a gentle piece of humor, closed after a single performance on Broadway. Like Owen, the play was out of its time. Considering what was happening in the country in the sixties, it had little chance for success. The critics, too, were searching for relevance. And it was probably as bad a play as they said. After that, fantasized love affairs, a distinctive consumption of alcohol, the body and mind disintegrating in a stupor. Given the life he had outlined for himself, he should have been riding in something grander than the A train when he was mugged. And he should have died of something more contemporary than pneumonia.

Owen, Stephanie, all of us, I suppose, wanted to buy into the system. At the same time, we wanted to occupy a distinctly private place in this world. A number were fairly successful according to the way we had been taught to measure success. We produced lawyers and doctors and Ph.D.'s and junior executives who by now have graduated into senior executives. We were eager to represent both the country and the dominant culture.

We, too, might have been thought of as activists. We wanted to get past our backgrounds, to deodorize all smells out of existence, especially the smells of immigrant kitchens and beer-sloppy tables.

A number of us had our reservations about "the American dream." There were just no alternatives to that dream that we could see. Some of us tried to hold on to the sentimental egalitarianism of the Jewish working class. That was finished, though, a fact that we had to recognize implicitly simply because we were in college. Rebellion had to be limited to verbal bravado, a show of contempt for the very Lady Success we worshiped. My friend Jack, the only other student I remember who called himself a socialist as a freshman, left Hunter after three years to attend Columbia law school, already engaged to a pretty, distinctly apolitical girl whose eyes were wandering from the Grand Concourse to the Riverdale palisades and beyond. When I was a graduate student at Columbia, I ran into him and we had lunch. He followed the stockmarket now and he carried the *Times*, and all during lunch he polished his glasses while he discussed the kind of furniture he and Alice were buying.

For my generation, home was really where the heart was. Of course, our America had made the heart, like the home, more mobile than ever before. We settled for what we could and mixed our successes and our failures. A few more have probably died, a few may have carved their names on the door and been tenacious enough to hold on to their dreams. Yet there were never any guarantees.

I am aware of the condemnation of my generation. Silent. And materialistic. We labeled ourselves so that no one had to perform that task for us. It is still difficult to feel passionate about the fifties; it is even more difficult to escape the sense of hypocrisy that lingers with memories of the decade. We condemn our mendacity of spirit to one another on the few occasions that we get together; we compare ourselves unfavorably to our own students who are, we insist, overflowing with generosity. They are not hypocritical, we decide. We were.

Many of our students tell us that America is a cesspool of corruption that cannot be cleansed until all the water has been swept out to sea. Our belief—perhaps I should call it hope—was that a man could get by, that he could turn inside himself with a bit of courage, and with silence, stealth, cunning, and luck manage to create an identity of his own. We were neither conquerors nor heroes. We survived in this world, perhaps less willing to take a chance than our students but perhaps less hysterical and paranoid also. We managed to differentiate between the public and the private selves, a feat that seems to me relatively healthy. We did not conceive of history as a plot. Despite the rise of a hysterical Right, we managed to keep our wits and to maintain a focus on our own problems.

We were not a particularly noble generation, nor did we have a vision of a coming paradise. We accepted technology in much the same spirit as we accepted the Cold War, as a fact of existence. Science, for us, was not Mephistophelian, for while we knew about the bomb, we knew about the Salk vaccine also. We insisted (undoubtedly naïvely) that science was neutral, and we voiced the inevitable platitudes about how man must use it for the benefit of the human race. We were suspicious of primitivism, accepting as a matter of course that it was better for peasants to wear shoes than to go barefoot. Our cars had not yet polluted the environment; they had, instead, created our mobility, which was more pleasing than we were ready to admit. We did not often challenge our teachers but we did remain skeptical and removed from what they taught us. We were not hero worshipers, for we had the experience of Nazi Germany vividly etched into our memory. A man like Kennedy was preeminently *our* politician, for his questioning, his sense of human limitations combined with his desire to steady affairs wherever they threatened to spin off uncontrollably, reflected the best we believed our world could expect. We would have instinctively resisted the appeal of a Che or of a Malcolm X or any public figure with "charisma." "Put your money where your mouth is" may not be the most startling profundity ever voiced, but it was a saying that represented the best that was in our skepticism. I wonder whether the present generation of college students is as free of cant and hypocrisy as it would like to think it is. We turned away from politics into ourselves, but it seems at times that this generation has made revolution into a business and is intent on commercializing passions that should remain private.

Our world was in a necessary transition. We lived in a country that saw the rise of the weekend bohemian who drove on Friday night from his Madison Avenue office to the White Horse bar in the Village to search for the personalities of art along with the college students. The sixties were to swap the bohemian for the radical who was intolerant of those who came to be called hard-hats. Ours was an ersatz Judaism, a world in which we would have settled for the rule of law; our students, I suspect, possess an ersatz Christianity when they insist on the rule of love.

I cannot speak of my education as inspired, and I will not speak of it as relevant. It did not pretend to what it could not accomplish, however. If I offer Stephanie's suicide and Owen's absurd death as the price some of us paid as we pried at the lid of the country's energies, I must also admit that their situations were not singular, that their stories can be found today. For us, men were neither devils nor villains. They struggled. And in our own struggle, a college education could still represent a significant step forward. I left college with a sense of accomplishment, a belief that there was a great deal worth knowing, along with an eagerness to know as much of it as I could. Henry Adams had complained that nineteenth-century Harvard failed him by seeking to make him a social being rather than a knowledgeable man. It may be that he (along with many of my class-mates at Hunter) received more than he had bargained for. The way in which the country conceived of educa-tion, as a power that could shape the course of one's rites of passage, shaped us at the same time that it placed new burdens upon our shoulders. Everyone had debts to be paid, even a generation of pragmatic Americans.

Chapter Two

In April, 1968, when Columbia University became the
focal point of the student disturbances that had originated
at Berkeley three years earlier, I would have been quite
happy to help anyone whose primary object was to level
Columbia to the ground. My reaction was so visceral
that it surprised even me, an expression of pure hatred
that rose from the wounded animal lurking within me. It
had, after all, been almost twelve years since I had departed Columbia with a deep sigh of relief and my M.A.
in English literature. It puzzled me that my contempt for
Columbia—for the feeling was probably closer to contempt than to hatred by 1968—should have lasted so
long, although I had been aware of its presence long
before Mark Rudd's reminder.

I assumed that my feelings would be shared by one or two of my colleagues at City, not by the dozen or so who turned out to be as spitefully enraged at Columbia as I. They, too, had put in time on Morningside Heights. Some, like me, had left as soon as they could escape with grace and an M.A. Others had continued on to the Ph.D. Columbia was a lingering taste of ashes on the tongue for the great majority of colleagues with whom I discussed the events of April, 1968. The school seemed to possess a peculiarly nightmarish quality for all of us. In the faculty lunchroom, there was a great deal of sympathy for the students, even among those teachers who ordinarily considered themselves conservative. The conservatism soon came to its own instinctive defense as the student challenge to the university became clearer. The initial reaction, however, was an undisguised pleasure at the sight of Columbia finally getting what most of us at one time or another had fervently wished for it.

The sins of Columbia could probably be discovered, in greater or lesser form, in most other high-pressure graduate institutions, which were undoubtedly equally overbearing and equally dehumanizing. The fact that it was Columbia that exploded can be attributed to a geographical accident, since it was not by choice or intention that Columbia looms over Harlem. Even in 1955, when I went there, the university felt threatened by its location. The contrast between the world of Columbia University and the world just beyond its boundaries was obvious to anyone who bothered to look, and it would take more than a gymnasium open to the public—even if the entrances were not separate—to ease the tensions. Why the worlds of Columbia and of Harlem should have been bridged is difficult to understand. It could have had little to do with Harlem's fabled vitality, for I had seen enough of it to know that whatever was bred in Harlem, kicks were not the chief product. Poverty is not particularly vibrant.

By the time I had spent a month in graduate school, I truthfully could not understand why anyone would want to claim those Heights. One did not have to romanticize ghetto life in order to find the puffy ostentation of Columbia unattractive. I find it difficult to envision a more lifeless, desiccated, and inhumane place than Columbia University in the academic year 1955–56. It was the embodiment of what the American academic community was suffering from in the fifties.

It is somewhat embarrassing to admit at this stage in my life, but I know that I approached Columbia with a certain awe. It is even less pleasant to recall I accepted without question the image of Columbia that had been provided for me by my teachers at Hunter, the majority of whom had done their own graduate work there. I suppose this simply shows that academics tend to look at their graduate schools as alumni look at their college football team. My teachers had warned me of the graduate school grind. I had been told that I would encounter a university that demanded a great deal of its students. I should not expect the kind of faculty availability that I had for the asking at Hunter. Columbia's graduate faculty was too busy, much too busy. The consensus among my undergraduate teachers was that the faculty at Columbia was engaged in some terribly significant occupation vaguely classifiable under the heading *research;* the faculty at Columbia was different, in spirit if not in kind, from the faculties at all other New York colleges, or so I was led to believe.

38

Only a few boys in my neighborhood had attended Columbia as undergraduates, either the recipients of some scholarship aid or else the offspring of parents willing to take on virtually any financial burden in order to send a son through Columbia. In our eyes, Columbia combined academic excellence with social respectability. The only close friend of mine who attended it as an undergraduate was a brilliant mathematician who soon began to identify not only his career but his very being with the idea of becoming a "Columbia man." He once dragged me to Baker Field to watch Columbia play Navy. I spent most of the afternoon gazing at him in astonishment as he pranced and shouted while we watched an exhibition of amateurish ineptitude that would have offended any twelve-year-old boy. But his prancing had nothing to do with football, a game he hated. He honestly felt the exhibition was necessary. It was his conception of what he had to do in order to turn himself into a genuine Columbia man. Trained to be doubting and intellectual, he was prepared to eat the sawdust of his dreams if only to emerge as a true believer.

Of course, the graduate school was removed from this kind of collegiate spectacle. I did not expect the style of my life to change drastically when I went there in early September. I simply arrived at Columbia convinced that it was an institution in which intellectual brilliance and spiritual dignity emanated from the very walls. Generations of scholars had endowed the school with a breadth of vision possessed only by the finest of universities. It seemed to me that this was the only true claim to importance a university could make. Here, I felt, I would share, through some mysterious symbiosis, in a tradition that upheld the power of imagination and the necessity of reason. The university I attended was so far removed from the university I dreamed of, though, that it made a travesty of my expectations.

When I ask myself exactly how Columbia failed me, I come down to three things: the faculty, the students, and the atmosphere that separated the university from its surroundings. I do not mean to exonerate myself from any blame, for if Columbia failed me, I must also admit that I probably failed Columbia. I certainly did little enough to help invest it with the kind of reputation it wanted. The university's failure strikes me as far more serious, since I had no illusions of being able to do very much for Columbia. If I had fairly high expectations of the kind of graduate education I wanted it to provide me, I was quickly disabused of them. At Hunter I had been expected to prove myself within the framework of a grading system that would label and certify me, like meat on the hoof waiting for the educated eye of the government inspector, but the system at Columbia seemed geared to the creation of an assembly line of scholars. And what it did to those scholars was frightening. For we *were* on an assembly line—only, instead of being expected to turn out a product, we were expected to work for that Grade A certification that would prove our qualifications, our ability to stand within the circle of scholars as ultimate equals. The task was made more difficult by the fact that none of us knew the extent to which we had to be certified or even by whom we were to be certified. Individual courses were not graded. A student wrote his thesis, passed a language examination in either French, German, or Latin, took his comprehensive examinations, and was ultimately awarded his M.A. in a first, second, or third degree. If one received a first—and very few were awarded—he was invited to remain at Columbia for his Ph.D. and was usually given either a fellowship or an instructorship at Columbia College; a second merely entitled one to remain at the university for his Ph.D.; a third meant that if a student really wanted to continue for his Ph.D., he would have to remove himself to some lesser institution.

Columbia guarded its own eminence. It remained distant, seemingly impregnable. Classes were large and depersonalized. At Hunter I seldom sat in a class of more than twenty-five students, but the course I took at Columbia in the literature of the seventeenth century was attended by more than one hundred students. Questions in class were rare. A graduate school fear seemed to have taken over; one learned to guard oneself; to ask a question in such an audience was to commit a purposeful act of defiance. The problem was to find another way of making one's individuality known, a way that would make personal contact less threatening.

The one exception to the impersonality of a Columbia graduate education was my thesis seminar, populated by no more than ten or eleven students. The teacher was an instructor completing his own Ph.D., a young folklorist and poet who had already had a book published and who was preparing his first volume of poems for publication. When I was in his seminar, he was not yet a success, although all signs pointed to his imminent arrival. He was forever telling us what Lionel had said to him or what Eric had said to him or what Bill had said to him. He was relentless in his attempt to impress us with the range of his acquaintance. On those few occasions when he managed to forget his need to belong to the gallery of scholarly eminence, he could be intelligent and persuasive, although he had already been turned to a delicate curve, a symbol hunter prowling a world populated by men who wrote books. He was what the critical profession called a myth man. He could bite with joy only into the wafer sun stuck in Stephen Crane's sky, as if there could be no sun without its being a wafer, as if Christ had succeeded for him, too, not in giving body and blood but in giving himself for literary form. There was no provincialism at Columbia; we knew about myth men and mythic criticism, and in my classes we crucified Christ again and again for reasons that undoubtedly would have appalled the early Christian fathers.

Our seminar instructor was expected to help us find a thesis subject, one considered worthy of examination by an aspiring M.A. candidate. He was also expected to impress upon us thoroughly the need for *research*. "What is it again you want to do your thesis on, Mr. Kriegel? Oh, yes, Orwell. Politics? Well, now, I'm afraid that's a little out of my line. We had that mingling of literature and politics in the thirties, didn't we? Of course, Orwell is an important figure. Fine essayist. Look, I'll tell you what. Why don't you run down to see Mrs. B.? She's the mentor for you." He was right. Mrs. B. turned out to be someone for whom politics had remained recognizable. She had been politically active during the thirties and spoke about the decade with affection. She would be happy to serve as my mentor, though, to be truthful, she didn't really care that much for Orwell. Or for his view of the Left. And the voice hedged just a bit as the old wars began to rise to the surface, and her face began to take on the lines of a hunger that she had suddenly been reminded of, if only for the moment. I liked her. She was one of the few teachers I was to meet at Columbia who thought of students as people rather than as categories.

Graduate students do not realize the extent to which the academic myth has seized its progenitors. What occurs to me in thinking about Columbia was the way in which a member of the faculty was wholly defined by what he had done, a phrase that meant what he had written. For writing and doing were one and the same thing. What he published became his identity—not, as with a novelist or playwright, because he had succeeded in giving life to a theme or to a character but because he had seized upon a particular intellectual terrain and had become identified as the man who had written "the definitive study" of some writer or movement. It did not really matter which writer, whether well known or obscure.

It would be incorrect to describe my teachers at Columbia as barnacles on the ship of art, although there were moments when I confess I thought of them as exactly that. Still I had to admit that they brought to their research, if not to their classrooms, an intellectual passion that was creditable. So many of them, though, had failed to retain the origins of that passion, and I was scornful of them for that. They had grown hungry in America, where culture, too, could be shipped and sold as a commodity, and when they sniffed the musty air of Philosophy Hall, they caught not the breath of dignity but the whiff of power. They knew the value of reputation, and they would bank it with all the fierce pride of Wall Street lawyers still fearfully aware of their tenement roots. The process of attaining a reputation was part of a Columbia graduate education, and we were exposed to it as soon as classes began. A man needed reserve and style and distance here; intelligence was not enough. It caused me a certain anguish that year, since I was not capable of approaching the world of arts and letters with the sugar-glazed propriety that was part of the proper psychic uniform.

The "name" professors, those faculty whose shoulders were burdened with the reputation of the department, possessed that distance and propriety. They possessed other qualities, too. Some of them possessed contempt for their students, which was puzzling at first, for in my naïveté I had expected to find men who were eminently pleased to be paid for teaching. I was soon overwhelmed with the inherent snobbishness that seems to attach itself to the humanities in general and to the study of literature in particular. Two professors of modern drama dueled each other for students, insisted on declarations of allegiance, of commitment not to a critical perspective but to themselves. Every man a king—or at least every full professor.

We were eager followers. How else to establish one's rights within the system? "You have to suck around a bit," said a fellow graduate student who had been an undergraduate at Northwestern. "First you decide what you're going to do your thesis in, then you try to get one of the important people interested in it. And in you. Even if he's not going to be your mentor, he'll put in a good word for you with one of the M.A. people." I didn't even know who the important people were when I arrived, although I knew the reputations of individual scholars on the faculty. I soon found out that importance was measured in terms not of scholarship but of power within the department. The best people, or at least the best scholars, were not usually interested in power. Certain teachers, however, were willing to look over prospective converts. "You've got to latch on to one. You've got to latch on and you've got to make him feel that he is the light of the world for you, focus and altar and godhead and his own apostle all rolled into one. There is *a* way. If the man you follow hunts symbols, then you scour the texts with him. If he has an orgasm for a Joycean epiphany, then you bless Dublin for a church." A Brooklyn friend put it another way. "If you want to be invited inside, then you have to get yourself an angle. You don't have the graces yet. You're not exotic enough. The crazier, the better. Style. Grab them with your style."

True enough. For the one approach the faculty respected was style. Nor was it necessary to imitate theirs; the idea was to develop an individual style. Every arched eyebrow, every puzzled expression, every quizzical smile portended something, and deciphering the code was part of the game. If two professors smoldered with resentment over some real or imagined slur years earlier, students entered the imaginary tournament, allying themselves with one or another faction. Groups formed and disappeared. Energies were concentrated on style.

The lectures I attended in the graduate school at Columbia were generally mediocre. Ideas were only for consumption in books, apparently. The professor of modern British literature wryly recited the material he had already published. During the first two weeks of the term, he ran through his repertoire of jokes, then began all over again during the next two weeks. Like so many of the teachers at Columbia, he was not particularly eager to be questioned by his students. I remember once following him after class, eager to pursue a question asked at the end of the period, only to find him impatiently hurrying away from me. "Look," he finally snapped, "I have to get to the library. Don't you understand?" I understood. In the scale of academic values, he was linked to his reputation. And his reputation depended upon what he could glean out of that library, not on what he could tell me. I was an academic hanger-on, as were all graduate students, not really his concern at all.

The caliber of teaching at Columbia was considerably more pedestrian than what I had experienced at Hunter. Other than Professor Frederick Dupee, I cannot recall a single teacher whose lectures struck me as consistently stimulating. There were, of course, moments of enlightenment and stimulation. Generally, though, lectures were delivered with benevolent regality. A sense of scholarship floundered lifelessly as the essence of the Socratic brew was boiled down to bibliographical recitation, lists of articles and books, the voice chanting like a preacher reading biblical genealogy. Even men whose books I had read and found stimulating apparently felt that the classroom situation was something to escape from as quickly as possible. Even those who had something to offer their students, with one or two exceptions, resented having to offer it. They mumbled unintelligibly down at the floor, searching for an audience between the cracks of the wood. They had read a great deal and understood a great deal, but the type of intelligence that seemed most characteristic of Columbia was waspish and constipated. Though my graduate school lectures may have provided few moments of true illumination, I should add that this, too, was a negative gift of sorts. I soon found myself so disgusted with my classes that I spent most of my days at the library. I did a great deal of reading, although none of my teachers attempted what might be called a critical synthesis.

Nor were my teachers particularly interested in the life of the department. By and large, the faculty had abdicated all administrative responsibility. The chairman, a remarkable woman, was a distinguished seventeenth-century scholar who did not so much administer as rule the department. I suspect that, had it not been for the formidable prejudices against women administrators in the academic world, she would have held one of the major administrative posts at the university. Her chief assistance in running the department was a secretary, a middle-aged woman whose power within the department was immense. Most of the graduate students I knew were quite openly terrified of her.

The secretary guarded the departmental inner sanctum, the chairman's office. Her job was to decide which students to admit into the chairman's office and which to reject. I knew many graduate students who raged uncontrollably because they had been unable to get to see the chairman. They spoke of the secretary as if she guarded the gates of heaven, but the fault was certainly not hers; she sought to give an overworked boss greater breathing space. Nor was it the fault of the chairman, who was an effective administrator. It was the fault of a faculty so busy defining itself and its work that it was content to take from the department a steady salary and the protective shield of prestigious anonymity, which liberated them from students but left them free to publish, to greet visiting literary dignitaries, to display social grace as well as intellectual wit, and to partake in the comforts, however mundane, of the American university structure. To keep the student in his place seemed to be the one unbreakable rule.

If a student had graduated from Columbia College and

had established a reputation while there, he found the road to greater glory already paved. He could then afford to gamble, for he knew who the players were and which cards they held. There were even moments when that student was consulted as a lesser oracle. A friend of mine tells the story of having been sent by the department to an eminent classicist in order to see whether his Hebrew was sufficiently good to be substituted for one of the other three languages prescribed for the Ph.D. The classicist was also a Hebraist. My friend entered his office to discover another graduate student there, a former Columbia undergraduate. My friend dutifully made his request, only to listen aghast as the classicist, his delicate hand stroking his goatee, turned to the other student and suggested that he help decide whether my friend's Hebrew was proficient enough for Columbia. "I wanted to choke him. I sometimes think I should have. Just pack the Ph.D. in then and there. But I had to finish. There was too much invested in it by that time. So I stood there, smiling like a puppet, wondering whether this wasn't one of those moments when murder is better than patience."

The other graduate student, of course, was not responsible; my friend describes him as having been embarrassed during the incident. Columbia, though, presented sycophantic behavior as one of the legitimate ways for a student to get ahead. The university wanted talent, but no one really knew what constituted talent, and neither students nor faculty was very clear about potential worth. The faculty viewed the university as an extension of its comfort. Productivity was geared to keep select employees happy.

I somehow felt that I had little in common with my

professors. We shared a commitment to literary studies, but this was a most limited equality, one that cast me as beggar for the academy's wisdom. And yet these men had battled other demons. Was it not the same Jacques Barzun who sat enthroned, along with W. H. Auden and Lionel Trilling, in the Madison Avenue *kultur* advertisements that I studied in fascinated disgust in the Sunday *Times* who had insisted on the university's allegiance to the values of intellect? Whatever I felt about those advertisements that made a cultural mannequin of the intellectual, his allegiance had consistently been given to that European conception of lucidity and intellectualism that remained an academic ideal.

Unfortunately, the very people who had once themselves been victimized by the academic status system now felt obligated to the system. They did not work to change it because it embodied a trial they themselves had undergone successfully. It should not have taken the events of April, 1968, to indicate to them how dissatisfied students were. Certainly, the penitent parade of faculty before the confessional box of television cameras would never convince anyone who had attended Columbia's graduate school that these men sincerely wanted "contact" with their students.

The graduate education I experienced at Columbia succeeded only in alienating students and pushing them to the point where they viewed both the discipline and the teaching profession with contempt. The graduate student refrain that I heard at Furnald Hall was a constant lament for the love of history or of literature or of philosophy, and the problem was to keep that passion alive in the face of a professionalism that threatened and intimidated the student. I still feel obligated to warn each of my students who leaves City for Columbia how dehumanizing the graduate school can be. Quite possibly it has changed drastically since the events of 1968. Based on my own experience, I view such claims skeptically. So many graduate students I knew, in so many different disciplines, complained of the same thing: Columbia had reduced intellect to a peculiarly narrow cynicism. The faculty, with few exceptions, regarded students as impediments to research, to expression, to knowledge.

And yet the faculty by itself cannot account for the vehemence of my feelings about Columbia. By and large, the faculty was perfectly willing to leave students alone, to bestow an indifferent recognition upon us. They begged to be regarded at a respectful distance. The quest for status at Columbia had been passed down from the faculty, however, and had invaded the very beings of the students. Never before or since have I encountered anything comparable to the massive neuroticism of Furnald Hall. The majority of graduate students who lived there were so caught up in the game, so victimized by their desire for careers, so willing to preserve a place at any cost at the side of some academic eminence, that their lives became mere extensions of the dehumanization of the university. It always seemed necessary to impress senior faculty; the words were measured, deliberated; the opportunities were spotted and the thrust home made as deftly as possible. Ability and style were one. There were recommendations to be secured, jobs to be discovered. A good word here or there might lead to the opening of doors. We emulated our models, working for the day when we, too, might claim professorial status for ourselves and might look at our students as we ourselves were looked at—worshipers at the shrine of making it.

We were true and natural Americans, we Columbia graduate students. Competition was the single law of life that we all acknowledged. Those who accepted a predatory approach to the world would have been perfectly at home in Furnald Hall. I cannot remember, even on neighborhood street corners populated by edgy adolescents, individuals who so highly valued the put-down. There were times when I sincerely believed that the sole purpose of intellectualism was to serve as a verbal blade designed to cut the world down to size. Ambition was pitted against ambition; man after man exerted himself in the effort to score points. "You don't want to make it with me because I'm black," said the tight-faced black to the equally tight-faced white girl at the table in the Lion's Den. He had the instincts of an expert. The women at Columbia were also worshipers of intellectual form, and what fate could be worse than to be labeled a bigot?

The belligerence was in the air we breathed. What good were you if you could not manipulate language to advance your own reputation? The Riker's restaurant across Broadway was the scene of dozens of encounters between bleary-eyed graduate students suffering not from studying but from searching long hours after their own egos. Subject matter was peripheral; the speaker was all that mattered. It was like street corner action, where everyone—bus drivers, cabbies, passersby—eagerly joined in, neighborhood heroes all, ready with a whip of the tongue for the quick put-down. Like boxers circling their opponents waiting for the move, for the right moment. I had enjoyed this game in my adolescence, had played it eagerly, because it was expected of me and there was little at stake. No one pretended to generosity; no one claimed truth as a prerogative. But the intellectual dozens played at Columbia lacked honesty. We did not even have the courage to admit our need to dominate.

Columbia was steeped in a defined system of rewards and punishments. The university created a silent concert of consent that made reality the denial of its own innermost urges. If there is such a thing as institutional schizophrenia, we suffered from it at Furnald Hall. Grown men approached the issue of their own advancement with all the fervor of biblical exegetes. For most of us, the academic world had promised a way in which we could ignore the lure of materialism. Unfortunately, we turned into the consenting victims of what we claimed to ignore. If a student wished to buy the academic world, then it followed that he had to buy the rest of America also. It was nonsense to pretend, as we sometimes did, that this existed only among students in the law school or in the graduate school of business. If anything, they had the advantage of not lying to themselves, since they recognized that their lives were molded by those factors that ruled the nation. Those of us in the humanities tried to pretend that we were immune from the moneyed ideal of America, but we discovered temptation strewn along the path. The country was now willing to buy us, too. The choices were made a bit more suspicious and more attractive. Was it really so terrible to think of "productive scholarship" as a means of advancement? And what if productive scholarship led, in turn, to "productive administration"? Wasn't it a natural evolution?

The Furnald Hall lobby shielded the astronomers and physicists and mathematicians who were going to turn this planet around. Their idea of a political discussion was to wonder aloud whether Oppenheimer should have been permitted to head the Institute for Advanced Study at Princeton after he had been tagged a security risk, and their patriotism was a question not of mind but of muscle. They had already sniffed out the greater glory of rockets and cobalt weapons and moon voyages; they could fantasize rings around Buck Rogers, but they did it all quietly, their voices reserved and dispassionate and mechanical. In Furnald Hall the voice of the future was to be heard. The world was chopped into separate and distinct categories. Everything we felt about human life, words such as *truth* and *dignity* and *knowledge*, was stripped to the bone-dry terror that lay within the statistics. We pretended to be power merchants. Although power no longer seems so enviable as its responsibilities become more difficult to handle, we graduate students wanted to appear as if we took a modicum of power for granted. Power was obviously attractive to physicists and lawyers, yet it was not something of which students in the humanities could be oblivious. We could insist that in the society in which power would be judiciously used, only the humanities provided a suitable base for decision-making. We did not actually believe this, but it was easy enough to pretend that the study of literature was crucial. It should have occurred to us that literature was appealing because it could not be crucial in society's scale of measurement. We simply had to endow our life's work with the pragmatic thrust. Change the world with Donne and Oscar Wilde. Why not? It was our own way of swimming in the mainstream.

My ambition was to be a teacher who could somehow help his students with the task of defining themselves through the study of literature. The physicists and engineers at Furnald could define themselves and their goals in more national terms, since they were certain that their careers would offer measurable dividends. Ambitious and hard-working, they assumed that power would gravitate toward them upon demand. The humanities attracted those on the peripheries, those who wanted to be around the world of intellect. Nobel Prize-winning physicists were beacons in the cool Columbia darkness. Statistics could be buried until catastrophe became not only inevitable but desirable. Who among us could question the beneficence of plastic, except an occasional wandering writer who could be dismissed as a bit crazy?

It was not only physicists and engineers who believed the world turned around the realities of function and power. Furnald Hall was populated by historians and sociologists and philosophers whose perspectives could shift from a bland conservatism to a bold exploitation of intellectual style. Style reigned at Columbia, as much among students as among faculty. It was almost inevitable that we would all manufacture a myth about ourselves, simply because the myth-making process was one in which we all willingly shared.

My friend Sandy did not actually live at Furnald Hall. Nor was he, I eventually discovered, actually a student at Columbia. But he managed to manipulate the graduate school mentality so adroitly that we all assumed he was to the manor born. He was an academic simply by virtue of his claim to the distinction. He was something more than a bright Jewish boy from New Jersey; he was Hollywood material, a claimant to the American throne, for he had remade himself into the perpetually precocious *enfant terrible*.

Sandy succeeded in doing what everyone at Columbia

wanted to do. He reinforced his conception of himself
at our expense, like Joseph standing unrecognizable before his brothers. His friends, myself among them, comprised a group for whom the power of intellect became
synonymous with possession and with worth. We all
played the same game, but Sandy appointed himself
general because he was most successful at it. Intellect was
the basis of our social success. Degrees, I.Q. numbers,
academic awards, what teachers had said about us, these
served as badges of identification. He was capable of
inflicting his lies upon us with impunity, for we were
ready to welcome them. I was suspicious by nature and
doubtful of most claims, but I accepted his because they
were voiced in the name of intellect. He claimed that he
was a genius. And there simply had to be some real live
geniuses on Morningside Heights. He proved his case by
becoming a hanger-on, a nonstudent who showed up
mysteriously in any lecture hall—physics, biology, English. He had physicists convinced that he was the next
Einstein, psychologists convinced that he was the next
Freud, and he had all of us convinced that he was
Columbia's own Leonardo, the last universal man. He
mirrored our collective ambitions. We preened for him
with even greater alacrity than any of us had ever
preened for a teacher, and yet, when I thought about it,
it was obvious that he did not possess the kind of knowledge he claimed. Most of the time he didn't really
know what he was talking about. But I was willing to
grant him immunity because I was as ambitious as he was.
What could I say for sure about the man's claims? What
could anyone say? I knew, of course, that he would chip
in to discussions of intelligence by citing an I.Q. number
that stamped him the foremost natural in a world of

naturals. And while that did not impress me as much as it apparently impressed my scientist friends, his feats of memory, as well as the manner in which he carried them off, certainly did. He was like a Salinger hero in his apparent indifference to Columbia's opinion. He treated Columbia with contempt, which was more than anyone else I knew at Furnald Hall, myself included, was then capable of doing.

We eventually discovered that he was not a student—he had, it developed, never graduated from college—yet this does not take away from his claim. He was our Columbia. Perhaps only a schizoid could recognize the essentially schizoid qualities of Columbia. Sandy's estimate of the school still seems valid. The graduate school was a destructive place, and perhaps the only way to face it with cohesive reality was to compartmentalize your soul, to insist that the real you, the essential person had nothing to gain or lose from judgments rendered there. Perhaps it took a schizoid to get beyond the personal hostility pervading the graduate school. If students today tend to confuse intellect and pretentiousness, the source of that confusion may very well be found in the way in which schools such as Columbia present intellect. Graduate students were scarred by the endurance contest of graduate education. Intellect at Columbia presented itself as heightened belligerence. The claims made in its name were too great to stand up under scrutiny. And so we all turned on the very values that had sent us to graduate school. I can think of no place where the world of ideas seemed less attractive to me than at Columbia, for what it did to both faculty and graduate students was apparent. A phenomenon like Sandy, for whom illusion and reality had fused to fashion the con artist, was far more successful in dealing with Columbia than I was. He simply did not let it affect him because he was able to manipulate before he could be manipulated. He used intellect as he saw it used at Columbia—as a weapon. He did not have to overvalue it.

Ultimately, the kind of experience that my peers and I underwent in Columbia's graduate school would send some of us into the line wanting to exchange Matthew Arnold for Jerry Rubin, to give up our training for the opportunity to let loose and scream. We would call for the circus in the name of mysticism or drugs or God knows what else. And the new gods would soon spread among us, eager to offer the faith even in the paneled lobby of Furnald Hall. The university will undoubtedly be forced to adapt under such pressure; even Columbia demands the contemporary. And it will probably survive, since it is geared to survival, a survival that it confuses with the survival of the values it claims to profess.

The community surrounded the college, threatening even then to envelop it. It was becoming unsafe to walk the streets at night in 1956. The danger was more talked about than tangible, but after darkness descended, the side streets had to be approached with caution. Anything was possible. Columbia had begun its attempt to ward off invaders. To the north it had erected a housing co-operative; throughout the area it was buying up buildings and tenements, evicting older tenants and replacing them with students and faculty. Columbia was learning and knowledge; it was also real estate, a subject no one wanted to discuss. The threat from Harlem was already obvious. Had the university administrators possessed foresight, they might have gone about things differently. And yet they were simply doing what every other major urban university did, trying to protect a geographic enclave. In America the city followed the university. Columbia possessed its sense of mission. Palliatives were bound to be local. And few in 1956 cared to predict the ultimate outcome of the black struggle. No one then carefully called Negroes "blacks"; Jackie Robinson was our image of black success. In any case, at Columbia we were all too busy trying to gain perspective and status; Blake and high-temperature physics were the tools of our craft. We had no time for the black ghetto.

I cannot remember ever hearing a word about Harlem or even about race during my nine months at Columbia. The Jews in the graduate school avoided all talk of race or nationality, intent on proving to themselves and to the world that they, too, were just Americans. There were a few guarded and unspecified references to "the neighborhood" in Furnald Hall conversations. The implications behind these remarks, though, would have been lost on anyone who did not know the racial composition of the surrounding neighborhood. The danger, or the potential for danger, was ignored. The university more or less denied the existence of the Harlem that could be found below the steps of Morningside Heights. Fear, like race, was also not discussed. Columbia would remain, or so it silently hoped, a democratic fortress, determined to keep itself clean for the future harmonious world. We students were willing enough to go along with so unthreatening a vision. When we encountered blacks in the Lion's Den, we were solicitous, ready to prove our liberalism. They were probably not students, but this was something else we did not talk about. There

58

were a great many things that we did not speak of at Columbia. I simply accepted Columbia's values and its conception of the neighborhood, although the school's beliefs were not my own. They just existed, like degrees to be earned, or the university catalog, or the small public library in the basement of Butler Library. There had been a time in my life when Harlem had been friendly territory, but the atmosphere at Columbia had made me wary of the neighborhood. What had interfered, I still ask myself, to breed such new fears?

It may have had something to do with our reverence of intellectual form, so often stripped of substance. The unspoken myth of our time was that cognitive power, the ability to think in abstract terms, had been denied the Negro. We were indoctrinated with the idea that black people could not think. Any child who had ever watched a shuffling Hollywood black rolling his eyes simply knew this for a fact. The only art that could emanate from Harlem was jazz, and no matter what verbal allegiance we might pay it, it remained inferior to the unalloyed products of intellect we had been trained to revere. Today we are simply turning the myth of the noncognitive black man inside out. The stereotype no longer shuffles; he still remains stereotype, however.

"You can't get wrapped up in history," said a student of mine to me recently. "It's aristocratic," he insisted, thus indicting the past absolutely. History threatened to rob him of his passion by confusing him, by insisting that he give his vision some perspective. He was going to "feel" his way through life; he was going to live spontaneously. And he believed in the equality of all men; he wanted that understood. It was a bland equality, though. He had no idea of what made men push their bodies against mountains. In a way, I almost prefer the old wars. This insistence that all men are brothers not beneath the skin but without skins reminds me too much of the silence we drew like a silken curtain across the subject of race at Columbia. It would have been better if we had talked.

My experience at Columbia convinced me that there are more attractive styles for the young to choose than to be a Columbia intellectual. I can understand why so many have turned away from the kind of choice my generation made. Today they doubt not their capacity to reason but the necessity to reason. Their music, their drugs, even their insistence on the visual over the cerebral seem to stem from their rejection of a false idea of intellect that we accepted too willingly. Columbia's graduate school remains fixed in my memory as a place that demanded the purgation of any good instincts a student had. The one-upmanship to which all graduate students at Columbia were exposed evokes a bitter memory. Perhaps it can be dismissed as a minor evil in a world in which real evil is so available. And yet I hope that I continue to retain the memory of that year within me, for it serves me well when I think of what I owe my own students. It was at Columbia that I first learned how dangerous the academic world could actually be. For it can destroy in the name of enlightenment and corrupt in the name of truth. Columbia did not kill its graduate students, but it bowed their heads more than a little.

Chapter Three

When I left Columbia, it was with the firm intention of never again setting foot in the academic world. As soon as I had vacated my room at Furnald Hall and departed with my books and belongings, I felt an overwhelming rush of the emotions I had kept controlled within me. The anger had been dammed up, layer upon layer, and now there was no reason to stifle it. I left with neither wealth nor reputation, not having been the recipient of a number one master's. I would have welcomed that opportunity if only because a recurrent fantasy of mine since midwinter had been to walk into the chairman's office in order to turn down the offer of a position at Columbia. But I knew that it was an empty fantasy as soon as I had completed my thesis. Mine was just another M.A. thesis, although I did manage to push it to completion with a kind of energetic desperation, so badly did I need to get out of Columbia that June.

Early in January I had applied for a teaching assistantship at New York University on the advice of a friend whose reaction to Columbia's M.A. program had been very much like my own and who had departed Columbia for N.Y.U., where, he claimed, life was considerably more pleasant. In February I was informed that I might come down for an interview with the chairman of the English department. From the very first, I liked N.Y.U., simply because it was different from Morningside Heights.

The interview itself was quick and seemingly without purpose. The chairman stared down at a manila folder, then looked up at me. He tapped the desk and pointed to the folder, which contained my transcript. "Fine recommendations you have here. Unfortunately, we don't have any positions available."

"Why did you call me down, then?"

"Oh, I liked your letter. And there's always the chance that something will open in September." With that, he offered me his hand and I left.

I felt some irritation but little regret when I learned that there were no assistantships available. By February I was eager to sever connections with the academic world and try my hand at something else. In June I took a job with a small publishing company, convinced that the academic world and I had split the sheets in what had never really promised to be a very lasting marriage for either of us.

At this stage, I am not at all sure what changed my mind. I had an interesting job and the salary I earned kept me from living like a student. When I received a

telephone call from N.Y.U. early in September, however, I knew that I was going to accept whatever was
offered. Living the life of a student would mean that I
would once again be forced to guard pennies, to manage
on a budget of about ten dollars a week (which is what
I had more or less lived on at Columbia). The salary
I was earning in publishing was not enormous, but it
had, at least, liberated me all through the summer of
'56 from graduate school penury. The American graduate
student exists in a society that is anxious for him to become a professional but is suspicious of his being an
intellectual.

The student assumes, and society concurs, that he is
a kind of parasite; he lives, he has been told by those
who have proudly graduated from the "school of hard
knocks," on the grudging charity of others. And so he
begins to consider himself to be an investment in the
future. He is not even able to differentiate between the
part of his future that belongs to him and the part that
belongs to society. He discovers that in graduate school
he is no longer willing to make the physical sacrifices
that undergraduates accept as a matter of course. In
short, his life leaves a great deal to be desired, especially
since he finds himself in a state of transition between
being an undergraduate and entering a profession. There
is no sense of possible action in graduate school. There
is a sense of ultimate purpose, but it does not provide the
physical impetus necessary to get through the days. My
salary as a teaching assistant would not be much com-
pensation for a return to graduate school. For a year of
teaching two freshman English courses per term, I was to
be paid $1600, along with free tuition for eighteen course
credits in the graduate school. Even at a time when
N.Y.U. was paying its senior faculty notoriously in-

adequate salaries, this salary was worthy of the sweat shop rather than the academy. And yet I accepted the offer immediately.

N.Y.U. was under no illusions about the nature and purpose of its destiny. Unlike Columbia, it did not even try to pretend that intellectual passion alone kept it in business. Central to all decisions was the rather elementary question of cost. Nor was I ever made to feel that being the recipient of a teaching position while working toward my doctorate was a singular academic honor, or proof that I had been called forth and chosen, which was how Columbia insisted on looking at such things. My thesis seminar instructor at Columbia had really believed that being permitted to rub shoulders with eminent academicians was ordination into the literary priesthood. He was a charter member of a class willing to exploit itself in order to pretend that it stood at the sources of power. To retain an imaginary dignity without admitting that the economic realities of academic life were exploitative was an illusion that seemed endemic to the situation of the young academician.

The Ph.D. candidate pledges his psychological and emotional resources to the prevailing academic system with the expectation of eventually achieving his own sense of fulfillment and a degree of power within that system. If he is successful, then one day he will rule the destinies of other aspiring Ph.D. candidates. His whims will then have to be placated; his desires for obeisance met; his opinions listened to, absorbed, incorporated into a student's work. The day will come when a candidate working under his tutelage will offer him services in any number of little ways. Small expectations, to be sure. But decisive.

When I broke down into dollars per hour the amount

N.Y.U. was paying me, it was evident that I was being exploited. I did not need Marx to tell me that. For teaching between one-half and two-thirds of a full academic load—and teaching it all in freshman English, probably the most time-consuming and difficult of all courses taught in the freshman year of college—I would be paid less than one-third of what an assistant professor received. Two classes of freshman English meant that I had to correct approximately forty-five themes per week, hold conferences with students about their writing, and attend weekly meetings at which the problems of teaching freshmen to write were discussed at length, not to mention preparing and delivering my classroom lectures. Of course, I could add to what I was being paid my eighteen tuition-free credits per year. However, it would have been no more difficult to continue in publishing and to pay for the credits. It certainly would have been financially preferable. Why, then, did I accept the offer of an assistantship?

My reasons will probably make sense to my peers in the academic world. I knew that I was placing myself at a financial disadvantage, but I also knew that, in working for a Ph.D., it would help me to be around the teachers I was working with. While I enjoyed my job in publishing, it seemed to me that I could always return to it. The true logic of my decision lay in the fact that I had adopted the viewpoint of the academic world once again. From the moment I answered the telephone, I had been brought back inside the fold.

I am among the few people I know who actually enjoyed his Ph.D. studies. Everything I have written about graduate education to this point, along with the automatic warnings I offer those of my students who plan to pursue a Ph.D., should testify against this. And yet I remember the four years I spent at N.Y.U. with a great deal of pleasure. In principle, N.Y.U. was no different from Columbia, except, of course, that it lacked Columbia's reputation. Columbia was probably among the five best graduate schools in the country in 1956, whereas N.Y.U.'s reputation can best be described as mediocre. The school had only a few graduate departments with established academic reputations. An influx of brilliant refugee mathematicians in the thirties had given it one of the best applied mathematics faculties in the country. The art history department was among the most brilliant faculties of its kind in the world. Both the English and history departments, in which I was to do my own graduate work during the next four years, boasted prominent scholars among their graduate faculties. And yet there was something disreputable about N.Y.U. Students who went there usually thought of it as a second choice; more often than not, they arrived there by accident rather than design.

I think it was N.Y.U.'s slight touch of raunchiness that made it so appealing to me. This was a university on the make, but its corruptibility was at least open. What other university, desirous of proving itself, would have built an expensive student center at the very time that its library could most charitably be described as comic? What other university could have been quite so cavalier as it took part in the systematic destruction of Greenwich Village? (Columbia, of course, tried to stave off Harlem. But no one wanted to preserve dilapidated tenements and seedy rooming houses. There the argument was that the neighborhood desperately needing housing facilities. The Village, on the other hand, had been the center of the very qualities in American culture that a great university might have been expected to protect and to nourish.)

The pervasive atmosphere of N.Y.U. was no different from that of America at large. N.Y.U. adhered to the rules that dictate the style of the successful operator. Of course, one might argue that Columbia was no different in this respect. But it was the very openness of its commercialism that set N.Y.U. apart. The casual manner in which a department chairman—*any* department chairman—would load extra students on the teaching assistants or the younger assistant professors or the older members of the faculty who lacked reputation in order to up the ante of some senior professor was universally accepted. The teaching assistants themselves simply looked upon such boondoggling as part of the professional hierarchy; their day would come. Chairmen simply rearranged schedules. The result was that a young instructor would discover another few students in his class, a rumored new teaching assistant appointment would disappear, and Professor X, who was just as at home in physics as he was in English, would decline another offer and come away a few thousand dollars richer. To the credit of N.Y.U., the school was not hypocritical; it looked upon the process as inevitable. No one, to my knowledge, pretended that transactions in the academy were different from what they were. The university was simply acting as an extension of the larger society.

The School of Commerce, at which I taught during my first term as a graduate assistant, set the tone for the rest of the university. The undergraduates regarded the "liberals" (by which they meant intellectual disciplines, not men or political parties) as obstacles to be cleared away before learning the mechanics of merchandising or accounting or retailing. They were not particularly good students, but teaching them proved both challenging and rewarding. Encouraging and helping them to read with diligence and intelligence was a formidable trial for any teacher. And it necessitated a confrontation with the myths that had been shaped by the academy itself.

I discovered this much later. My first revelation was that the School of Commerce was N.Y.U.'s statement of intent, in certain respects the soul of its being. No doubt the dean insisted that his prospective businessmen all have the proper smattering of culture. And why not? Given where we were and what we were doing, given what America had claimed for itself in the twentieth century, then what right did I have to challenge the right of retailers and merchandisers to put in their bid for Plato and Shakespeare? Would America not be well served in this manner, too?

No humanists could have been more devoted to the idea of the "well-rounded man" than were the teachers of retailing and merchandising at Commerce. I am convinced that no one has greater respect for the achievement of the intellectual, no one is more willing to listen to the wisdom that intellectuals can offer, and no one has a greater sense of formal obligation to the past than these same retailers and merchandisers. They may remain oblivious to the uses of intellect, but they hunger for admission to the club at which the products of intellect were on display. And since they had created the wealth that art needed in order to survive under capitalism, their demand that a few of the edges be rounded off in order to shape the inner man was natural and understandable.

The veneer of Columbia had driven me half crazy; at that institution I was supposed to pretend that the true power of the academic world was the power of learning. N.Y.U. required no such pretensions. On my first morning as a teaching assistant, I wandered through the halls of the School of Commerce, stopping first at the student lounge on the ground floor, named after an All-American tackle who had, I assumed, between leading the blocking on power thrusts through the line, been a student in these halls. Then I took the elevator to one of the upper floors and found myself wandering through refurbished display stalls. The scene resembled a modernized and strangely deserted Orchard Street push-cart entrepreneurship with all the combinations of the plastic rainbow, now emptied of merchandise and filled instead with neatly typed cards of retailing instructions. It was important, I discovered, to create a blending of display colors that appealed to the customer, and it was the responsibility of those who sold the goods to induce pleasure in the customer at the prospect of his purchase. The logic was impeccable. As my students would soon inform me, at the prices N.Y.U. charged, certification was necessary. Diplomas, too, were commodities.

Students at Commerce assumed that the business school supported the rest of the university. The assumption was natural enough, since their classes were so large that it was logical to believe that the university made a great profit from them. The first freshman English class that I taught at Commerce numbered more than thirty-five people; comparable classes at Washington Square College had between twenty and twenty-five. Strangely enough, the large classes didn't annoy the Commerce students. They accepted the fact that the business school func-tioned under less than desirable conditions, perhaps in order to prepare them for that "dog-eat-dog" world that they invariably mentioned in their themes. The elevators filled to bursting with sweating, straining students, each of them jockeying for position with elbows flaring and briefcases held like bludgeons. The street boy's style was an unexpected asset among these young men and women. Such was the knowledge that Commerce offered, as well as a smattering of Plato and those plastic cases in the corridors that illustrated the rudiments of retailing and merchandising. Gifts of the mind and heart. These young men and women accepted Plato as they accepted the elevators, one more trial that N.Y.U. had in store for them before it was willing to grant them certification. The system could be made to pay off later; these students understood the statistics that told them exactly how much a college degree was worth in cash. It was all open and aboveboard; if part of the problem of success was to read Plato and pass a quiz on the meaning of the cave myth, then they would read Plato and pass that test.

Their respect for literature was greater than I had been led to believe, since one of the lessons that America had taught them was the worth of endurance. I have never taught *The Iliad* to a class more eager to grant the work's greatness than the class I taught that first semester at Commerce. They were immensely pleased to be reading a book that had endured for so long. The life of a book became synonymous with its worth. Perhaps because of this, they attempted to respond favorably to the traditions that stood behind all the years Homer had lasted.

In large part, the educational process at Commerce consisted of applying thin layers of "culture" to these young men and women, most of whom were already convinced that they were not worth educating. Despite their belief in their own intellectual inferiority, they were anxious to consume all of the prescribed material. I was teaching a class at Washington Square College at the same time that I was teaching a class at Commerce. The students I taught at Washington Square were undoubtedly "brighter," but the students at Commerce were more open, more immediate; they had not been subjected to the educational experimentation that went on at the Square. Neither students nor administration nor faculty at Commerce was eager to rock any boats, certainly not any cultural vessels. In the Square, on the other hand, the new god had already emerged in the form of closed-circuit television, and men were already working to carve out careers as McLuhan's *technische Korps* even before McLuhan had been heard from.

Many college teachers assume, for some unfathomable reason, that the television screen is endowed with some sort of totemistic magic, that it ensures instant relevance through its manipulation of highly charged air waves. It was obvious to most of us who were teaching assistants that the use of closed-circuit television lectures was primarily designed to cut down on the university's payroll. College teaching was no longer the gentlemanly profession it once had been, and even we had to recognize that colleges were going to have to find some way to hold on to their senior faculty while, at the same time, they would have to service large masses of students. The most logical, or least expensive, solution was to increase the number of poorly paid graduate assistants, place them under the nominal supervision of an older, more experienced member of the department, and combine their classes with large public meetings at which the television lecturer would try to bring the syllabus together. As far as the students in the classroom were concerned, the experiment proved a disaster. I would discover half of them nodding away in their seats while the lecturer illustrated how to write a theme with his pointer jabbing against the magnified paper on the screen. The television lecturer tried hard to keep his audience's interest; the fact was that freshman English was simply too difficult to teach over a screen. A student and teacher who met and worked together on the problems of writing needed no third party's interference. My students were even more confused after discovering that much of what they had been told by that face on the screen contradicted what I had been telling them. In education, however, experimentation is supposed to justify itself. The business of learning demanded that we embrace the electronic goddess and that we voice extravagant claims for her miraculous powers. Never mind that the students went to sleep. Never mind if this experiment destroyed rapport between teacher and student. Every emperor chooses the clothes with which to cover his nudity. I am willing to bet that there exists a justification of that closed-circuit class somewhere in N.Y.U. The academic world is a sucker for the modern.

Washington Square College attracted an unusual student population for a New York school: would-be New Yorkers from Ohio, excited by the idea of living in the Village, young women from Forest Hills whose idea of a college education had a great deal to do with who had been pinned that week and what their own marriage expectations were, a few scholarship students selected through a system that was rumored to favor non-New Yorkers, a few ex-servicemen who had decided that a college education was a necessity. The Square also gave me my first look at a student who was to become more familiar as the years went by: the wandering student drop-out. At N.Y.U. there were few of these students around, but they were exceptionally bright and aware. (As the drop-out has grown more fashionable, he also seems to have become less intelligent. In the fifties, his position was more singular than it is today.)

The students whom I liked best at Washington Square College were dubious about what a college education could do for them and even more dubious about what they were seeking from that education. Usually they were older than other freshmen; some of them were ex-servicemen who had bought the idea of attending college with great reluctance; sometimes they were men in their late twenties or early thirties who had drifted from job to job and who now discovered that they wanted success, that they needed to do something different—intent on purchasing just a bit of the nation's commercialism but intent, too, on retaining the private self, the person who had become a stranger to many of their younger peers. I can summon up almost all of them from memory, but Duke comes to mind first.

Duke was already in his mid-thirties when he walked into my freshman English class. He was broad shouldered and squarely built, with big hands and a body like a wrestler's. His first theme immediately set him apart, not only in his articulate handling of language but in the experience he was able to call upon. During the term, we talked a great deal. Most of our conversations took place in the Chock Full O'Nuts across the street, where Duke would accompany me when I went for coffee after class. He was a cop and he had to schedule all his classes before one o'clock so that he could get down to Centre Street headquarters, where he held down a desk job.

Other than his curiosity, he had no reason at all for being in college. He claimed that he wanted to try his hand at writing, although his ideas about it were a bit vague and unformed. A capable writer, he was on the verge of creating an individual style when, during his senior year in college, he gave up writing to spend weekends as a ski bum. I suppose he never took the idea of being a writer seriously, although I have rarely met a student more appreciative of the talents of others or more responsive to good writing. He was more intelligent than the other students in class, but with enough experience so that intelligence in isolation did not overwhelm him. So many younger students who were intelligent couldn't handle it, didn't really know what to do with it, and so they tried to remodel themselves, to emulate those professors in whose wit or sensitivity they discerned approval and sympathy. Duke possessed distance, and this permitted him the assumption that all men were intellectually hungry. His approach to life was one that often makes teachers nervous, for the students who upset us most are those who really do take their intellectual independence for granted.

I liked teaching Duke, although I alternated between admiration for the fact that he did not seek to define himself through his education and annoyance at the casual manner in which he approached his work. On one hand, I believed in encouraging the independent mind; on the other, I was already enough of an American to insist that action had to possess a certain moral value. And moral value had to be visible in order to be recognized.

74

Duke wanted only the education of the private self. Years later he said to me, "What you couldn't understand was that I wanted to retain my amateur status. There are enough writers in this world. Look, I love to ski. But I don't have to write about skiing in order to justify myself."

George was another student I remember well. He was in Duke's class. He was my own age, twenty-three. He had lived on the Lower East Side, worked for a year after he finished high school, then enlisted in the air force, since he had nothing better to do. He found himself as confused and uncertain about his future on the day he was discharged as he had been on the day he enlisted. He came to N.Y.U. because he had no other place to go; he knew nothing about Washington Square College; he knew nothing about any college. He kept on talking about the fact that he had no idea of what he wanted to *do* with his education and never questioned the idea that it was imperative to do something with an education. His confusion was genuine; he was not equipped to handle the pragmatic ethos. At the same time, he had not come to college merely to *major* in one or another subject; his mind was still geared to the idea that college was intended to fill some intellectual void in his life. As time passed, he grew disconsolate and guilty about his lack of a goal. No matter what I might say to him, there were too many authorities telling him that he had to want to *be* something, to perform some specific task in life. Deans, counselors, even his fellow students all urged him to declare himself; a man was the work he performed. We believed not so much in the intensity of work as in its capacity to define one's life. There was something concrete about studying to be a doctor or a lawyer or a

75

teacher of Japanese. The desire for education alone might be creditable in the abstract, but unless it was anchored to some specific goal, it was suspect.

I was more tolerant of educational goals than I would admit. Students needed them; the inability to define their goals could swamp them by making them feel purposeless. Today, the situation is reversed. Some students strangle in confusion and boredom because they have never really permitted themselves to think about doing anything and because, when they speak of what they want for the future, they tend to think of it as an abstraction; usually they talk about the future by talking about freedom. Freedom, as they speak of it, seems to be a synonym for a nonverbal response to an all-encompassing world. They have decided that education is irrelevant to their needs and desires even though they have few desires that they can articulate and their needs are strangely passive. Frequently they become boring in the very act of insisting that school does nothing but bore them.

There may be a great deal to be said for the desirability of working toward a goal and even for demanding that a college education address itself to the demands of an eventual vocation. However, a student should be encouraged to explore his world as fully as possible; he should not be made to feel that the greatest of academic sins is not knowing what trade or profession to follow. Nor should he be made to feel that his education can be justified only vocationally. I am not arguing here for a return to the academic gentleman. Our universities no longer serve the constituency of those with excessive leisure time looking for the proper polishing. I am not arguing for a community of scholars absorbed in prob-

76

lems that have nothing to do with that which lies beyond the university's gates; this country can well do without either constrictive idea of what an education should be. However distorted its function may at times appear, a university's primary reason for being is to permit minds to develop their own potential. We cannot achieve a university that is nothing but intellectual, but we should not surrender to the mixture of certification factory and research institute so characteristic of contemporary American education. There must be a surer ground for a university to occupy, a place that does not ignore legitimate political demands of the day but a place whose fundamental loyalty is to its students. For it is only in the students that the university finds its own liberation.

Like most other colleges, Washington Square scrutinized the student carefully and judged him as if he had intentionally presented himself for examination. The student's participation in education was not denied; his individuality, on the other hand, was. Distance from students was imperative; in itself, this might have been healthy, but the distance called for was clothed in a pragmatism that had little to do with the teacher's real needs. Here one looked at students only insofar as they brought credit or discredit to the college. The chief function of a student adviser was to keep the school free of trouble. Any potential troublemaker was watched for fear that he would in some way dishonor N.Y.U. I remember an incident in which one of my students was sent to a school psychiatrist. She advised him to commit himself to Bellevue, which he did, only to be released two days later because his "breakdown" turned out to be a case of physical exhaustion. I went to speak to the doctor the day after the student entered Bellevue. I encountered a woman who obviously did not like what she was doing, for she had been given the task of protecting the university, not the student. She was annoyed with my visit and immediately wanted to know my rank. Was I a professor? No, I was only a teaching assistant. Mr. A. was a student in my class and I wanted to find out what was wrong with him.

There was nothing I could do for Mr. A., she brusquely informed me. There had been, in her professional judgment, a distinct possibility that Mr. A. might do something that would reflect discreditably on the university. There was also, I interrupted, the possibility that Mr. A. might be hurt by committing himself. He had not seemed particularly sick to me.

"Are you questioning my judgment?" No, I assured her. I was only questioning whether Mr. A. really should have committed himself. "Let me remind you, Mr. Kriegel, that I am paid by this institution to keep it a healthy place for all. As far as I am concerned, he belongs in a psychiatric ward for observation. That's all there is to it."

I retreated with whatever dignity I could retain. I couldn't really have done anything else. Her assumptions and my imposition were equal in the academic world. She was certified and I was not. The doctor and my students understood this; I was just beginning to catch on. We could not meet as equals concerned about a student's fate until I had my Ph.D. In questioning her decision, I had, however unconsciously, attacked her status. I was untitled in a land of titles. A difficult prospect for her to face and a necessary one for me to accept at that point in my life, given the circumstances.

From the point of view of the college, students did

not exist as individuals. When they offered no "trouble," they were acceptable. When they did as they were told, defined a major field of study and some "worthwhile" future ambition and paid their fees, they were acceptable. If they won awards or recognition for the college, they were even more acceptable. Expected to keep in line, they were treated with a paternalism that was more absolute and less benign than administrators and teachers thought. I suspect that students were not altogether real to those smiling, hearty deans. Or to the doctors who preserved the school's normalcy.

My focus at N.Y.U. was not so much on my experiences as a teacher as on the process of acquiring a Ph.D. A graduate student who served as a teaching assistant was neither fish nor fowl. He was at the same time a student pursuing a course of study and a teacher employed by the university to liberate its more valuable members from the pains of teaching freshmen. As a teaching assistant, I was a member of neither the fraternity of teachers nor a member of the fraternity of graduate students. When I identified my interests with the students, I was constantly made aware of the power of faculty. My position made the needs of that power very clear to me. I shared an office with men who ruled my fate as a graduate student. This gave me an advantage over the graduate students who were enrolled in part-time programs by making me identifiable to the men who taught me.

We all had the sense of participating in a large, unruly family, and this was one of the virtues of N.Y.U. The physical conditions at the school were haphazard. The office was a huge unpartitioned room known as the "bullpen," which swarmed with teaching assistants, student helpers, secretaries, some prominent critics and scholars, and people who were just wandering in and out of the room. It was far better than the quiet cruelty of Philosophy Hall. Given such conditions, it would have been presumptuous for N.Y.U. to take itself as seriously as Columbia did. No one here saw himself as a guardian of the culture, and this helped make it a less uncomfortable place than Columbia.

The bullpen not only accommodated us, it forced us to live with one another. It was, of course, not particularly functional when it came to holding conferences with students. It was difficult to speak to a student with twenty other conversations, some of them more interesting than your own, going on at the same time. Luckily, the Village provided alternatives. In spring and early fall, there was Washington Square Park, where conferences could be held on a bench, occasionally interrupted by the park bums who wanted to talk about "how Tom Wolfe would've done it." In bad weather, there were enough luncheonettes and cheap restaurants around to serve the same purpose.

N.Y.U. was intent on improving its image. It was a university on the way up, eager to carve itself a substantial reputation. And in the process of achieving that reputation, classes grew larger, and conscience was assuaged by assigning some unimportant associate professor to supervise the work of the teaching assistants. We were expected to absorb his experience, yet each of us knew that his was the experience of failure. He had not added to the department's national reputation; he had given the school nothing beyond himself.

I never discovered among the faculty the contempt for

students that seemed so characteristic of Columbia. (It would come but not until after I had left.) Instead, the faculty was somewhat cowed by the students and seemed uncomfortable with its own authority. There were few people who saw themselves as commanders of the academic ranks. On an undergraduate level, there was the associate professor who had not achieved a scholarly reputation, who was not a particularly astute critic, who moved few hearts as a teacher, who had never held an important administrative assignment. He taught his classes, met his students, was cordial and considerate to all newcomers to the department, and managed to get by on a salary that would have infuriated a steelworker or a butcher. Usually he came from out of town; more often than not, he had arrived at N.Y.U. as a graduate student himself. Early in his career, a young Ph.D., he had been promising—a long article in a "reputable" journal, a review in *Partisan*. And since then he had settled into the comfortable if pecunious life of the academic who remains in the background, the man who commands neither fellowships nor sabbaticals nor raises and who soon thinks of himself as a hanger-on clinging to the peripheries of academic respectability. He was not in the same league with those whose names he dropped, trying to sound casual, whose reputations seemed to provide him with an endless source of conversation.

He was the man who paid by observing the success of others. And he had paid his entire life. The debts the university exacted from him were those that, within the turmoil of his mind, he could not feel were justified. Envision a man of fifty or fifty-five, balding, rimless glasses, the potential angular harshness of the face partially erased by time and the sullen acceptance of disappointment. Between those lips that did not have the courage to mock, a pipe clenched as a vestige of respectability. This man, no matter how long he roamed the streets of Greenwich Village, was doomed to be a perpetual outsider, a native of Ohio farms or Appalachian hills or the flat industrial cities of Michigan. He had not written, at least not in a long time, a fact of which he was reminded when salary discussion came around each year. He was not particularly popular with students, he had not built up a following. Not that anyone could deny that he had done his job. Still. . . . He had not even succeeded in his small chance at administration, and while it was never mentioned, both he and the chairman knew that his weekly sessions with the teaching assistants, in which he discussed their problems in teaching freshmen, bored the assistants and embarrassed him. They were as dubious about the value of his experience as he himself was, and they would listen to him mumble, "I'm afraid I don't know the answer to that one," a bit sorry for him as his teeth ground down on the stem of the briar pipe.

His refuges were sporadic. He had, if you could uncover it, a genuine affection for younger teachers and sincere sympathy for their problems. A few times each year you might find yourself sitting next to him at the Chuck Wagon for lunch, and then, quite unexpectedly, the two of you would discover that he did have something to say about his life as a teacher, usually the kind of gossip that was pleasant to listen to and that might, under happier circumstances, have produced material for an honest journeyman novelist. Stories about Thomas Wolfe at Washington Square, about teaching during the depression, about how he had come here as a young instructor, fresh from a small denominational college in the Midwest, to work for his Ph.D. He had all the scars that line the memories of Americans, and nostalgia made him yearn for the past as it faded into the distance. It had been better for him then, the world had not been so unaccommodating. "I remember when you could still walk to the fountain and see Cummings or one of the others. The first day I arrived in New York, I saw Dos Passos on MacDougal Street. It wasn't like this then." For his own life, he admitted, had taken a different turn from what he had once expected. "I bought a little place in the Berkshires. Just after the war. We bought it for the summers, my wife and I, but now we're thinking of putting in heat and modernizing it. I'll tell you the truth, Kriegel, I don't find New York as exciting as I once did. When I first came here, it was like being at the center of the world. Now I don't know. It's getting a bit too much for me. I'm getting old." And the inevitable nodding head.

Both of us knew that it wasn't a question of getting old. It was simply being forced to acknowledge failure, to recognize that the plans were stillborn and long since dead. He would never have the pleasure of walking into the chairman's office with a letter from another university asking whether his services were available. Year after year he would be faced with an inadequate raise or else no raise at all because there simply was no money for him. This disappointment would always be accompanied by the chairman's suggestion that if only he could tell the dean that *the* book was nearing its completion and had been accepted by a respectable press for publication, more money might be available. He would never write that book. Both he and the chairman

knew it. For the book itself was no more than an idea
that had years ago, perhaps decades ago, flickered on
the edges of his consciousness, until he had actually
seated himself in the library and pored over journals
and books and wondered whether he "really had anything new to say about the Elizabethans, anything that
has not been said before. Of course, no one recognizes
the value of publication more than I do. I'm not really
sure why. Somehow I've never been able to justify the
energy to myself. I wonder whether I shouldn't have
tried fiction instead. I guess I'm like all English teachers.
Fiction's what I wanted to do. That's where a man like
Wolfe had us all. He went ahead and wrote. We didn't.
Of course, he was compulsive. I'm sure you've heard
those stories. Why, I can remember visiting his apartment once, and the floor and the tables and the chairs
simply piled high with pages and pages of writing,
and . . ."

To be expendable was as unhappy a fate in the
academic world as it was anywhere else. This world
could be harsh when it dealt with questions of reputation. Even the graduate student was of greater interest
to the men who advertised the name of the department
than the associate professor simply waiting for time and
failure to pass. The graduate student, after all, might
yet go on to write his book.

I frequently wonder why I remember my graduate
school experience at N.Y.U. with affection. Was it
actually better than what I had experienced at Columbia,
or was it simply that, by the time I reached N.Y.U.,
I had already been exposed to the graduate school virus
long enough to have acquired some immunity? Still, there
were certain real improvements in my lot. I lived some-

what better than I had at Columbia. And while I have written about the teaching assistant as being exploited, I was always rather fortunate at N.Y.U. During my second year there, one of my duties was to serve as the reader for a well-known playwright, a job that made my life considerably easier, although it also led me to swear that I would never let anyone else grade papers for a course I was teaching. My third and fourth years were even less strenuous, since I was relieved from all teaching duties by fellowships that enabled me to study for my oral examinations and then research and write my dissertation.

N.Y.U. possessed other advantages. I enjoyed being in the Village, which still offered more than its share of good inexpensive restaurants, secondhand bookshops to browse in, a usable Washington Square Park, and a population that was still speckled with Villagers rather than legions of wandering teeny-boppers who invaded it in the mid-sixties. All of this was peripheral to my enjoyment of being a graduate student. My relationship to the university was the important factor, and from the very first, it was more pleasant than my relationship to Columbia had been.

Here is where the memories prove to be trickier. The graduate school about which I am writing has, I suspect, all but disappeared by now. N.Y.U. desperately wanted what Columbia had. Soon after I left, it acquired a dynamic young president capable of shaping his moods to whatever wind was currently blowing in the nation. The spirit of the place became constricted as the bullpen gave way to air-conditioned offices with pastel walls. N.Y.U. soon succeeded in turning itself into a lesser carbon of its Ivy League neighbor uptown.

I have no desire to exaggerate the virtues the school

possessed when I studied there. The quality of instruction was superior to that which I found at Columbia, but this is not particularly noteworthy; I can scarcely see how it could have been worse. The faculty was definitely more approachable, took greater pleasure in teaching, and did not regard graduate students with overt contempt. But N.Y.U. was also fragile and rather chintzy as a school; even then, it openly acknowledged being a university on the make. Although its prospects were in the future, its allegiances were happily still immediate.

Because the school lacked the basic amenities and facilities, the faculty somehow became crucial in the eyes of the students. The school's atmosphere always seemed to be shifting in accord with the needs of the students and faculty. It had many facets, at times integrating us in a hustling informality, at other times crippling us as the university regressed into a glorified training institute. Sometimes I suspected that N.Y.U. had absolutely no idea of what it wanted from its graduate students or its graduate faculty. This was actually a distinct advantage for those of us in the graduate school. We didn't take it too seriously, in large part because it didn't take itself too seriously. And no graduate school could be "first rate" without worrying a great deal about whether or not it was "first rate."

I was also fortunate that I chose to do my Ph.D. in American studies rather than in English literature at N.Y.U. I write this at a time when both the country and the culture have become less than fashionable in the academic world. At Hunter, and to a lesser degree at Columbia, I had listened to those who dismissed the worth of American life out of hand. The standard cocktail party line was "What civilization?" Time compounds the irony. Professors who once looked with horror at the interdisciplinary study of American life now bend with the pressure of fashionability: an excellent illustration of the ability of academics to discover "truth" in dark corners.

American studies is unfashionable today because it brings to mind an intellectual chauvinism that has been held responsible for its inception. It arose following World War II and reached its peak during the fifties, an evolution that has made it highly suspect, given the current political atmosphere of the academic world. Where it was once attacked only by conservative academicians, it now finds itself under fire from both Right and Left, from the first because it is not a "traditional" discipline, from the second because it has been associated with American "cultural imperialism."

I took my Ph.D. in American studies rather than in English literature because it seemed imperative to make sense out of the country in which I lived. Even American literature had not come alive for me, either at Columbia or at Hunter. I had, of course, read Hemingway and Faulkner and Farrell as an undergraduate, but my professors had taught me to view the idea that this country possessed either a culture or a civilization with suspicion. America possessed the momentum of its own energy, an energy that remained Manichaean as far as the house of intellect was concerned.

By the time I was a senior in college, I could speak with some knowledge about English Gothic architecture and Chaucer's poetry. I had never been to Cambridge, but I could recognize King's College chapel in my sleep, although I drove through New York oblivious of its architecture, unimpressed by anything that could be labeled American. By the time I completed my M.A., I felt less and less satisfaction with the limited vision of the "Eng. Lit." mentality. It seemed so constricted, devoid of the substance I was looking for, one that would help me discover a personal base from which to frame my own critique of America. It was also obvious that the study of English literature could be a mannered refuge, a pretense of mind.

I wanted to learn about America because the country truly puzzled me. I could not understand why it hadn't become either the dream or the nightmare that one felt it had been on the verge of becoming time and time again. I was warned by friends that it would be difficult to get a job with a Ph.D. in American studies. I knew how limited my patience had grown, however, and I had many reservations about my ability to push through to a Ph.D. in English. At N.Y.U., I could take advantage of a faculty in which both the English and history departments were strongest in their American branches.

In a sense, I was beginning a completely new field of study, and I enjoyed doing my Ph.D. because of this. I came to American studies from an academic background concentrated in English and European literatures as well as philosophy.

At a time when the traditional academic disciplines are under fire, my own experience indicates that the fire is at once justified and excessive. A student could do worse than to move into different areas when he does graduate work. Still, unless an interdisciplinary curriculum offers intensive work in the studies it encompasses, it is vulnerable to the charge of a lack of intellectual precision. The question of methodology, which is what American studies is said to lack, seems to me less important than the question of intellectual intensity. And intensity cannot be communicated by the field of study alone. At N.Y.U., I was particularly fortunate that the two men who ran the graduate program in American studies were Henry Bamford Parkes and Oscar Cargill, both of whom insisted that it was vital to master the delineations of American history and literature before presenting oneself for the Ph.D. examinations. An energy of mind and a mastery of basic material were necessary. History and literature possessed no single methodology; an eclectic criticism offered the best perspective to make sense out of the country and its culture.

Unlike Columbia, the graduate school at N.Y.U. could not afford the great put-down. The university lacked the power to dehumanize students because it was not prestigious enough to threaten them. There was a great deal of discontent among graduate students everywhere in the late fifties; much of their energy was defensive, just as it had been at Columbia. The atmosphere was healthier simply because we did not take it personally. We were all aware of how difficult the orals were supposed to be (at one point, nine consecutive candidates in English failed them), just as we were aware of the extent to which we were expected to become productive scholars and so justify our choice of professions. At the same time we were also aware that the process through which one acquired a Ph.D. was, in some respects, merely a game. The rewards at N.Y.U. were not great enough for anyone to take them seriously. Students seemed more human, less tense, than they had seemed at Columbia; they did not fit so easily into carbons of professorial dignity. Their conversation lacked that nervous dedication to self that I had found so often in Furnald Hall. The academic success at N.Y.U. cut a less imposing figure than his Columbia counterpart. Perhaps it was not really possible to be imposing in converted warehouses and office buildings. There was no way in which I felt that N.Y.U. could control my destiny, and I soon discovered that I did not have to be on guard against it as I had been at Columbia.

There was an absence of any real academic tradition at N.Y.U., and this would be considered a deficiency by most. Neither the faculty nor the student body was anchored to the university; the way out was always clear. Many of the graduate students attended N.Y.U. on a part-time basis. Columbia strongly discouraged part-time students, insisting that the stringent obligations imposed by graduate school could not be met on a part-time basis. No one mentioned that such a policy discriminated against students who could not afford to attend graduate school full-time. N.Y.U. was willing to accommodate graduate students part-time; classes were offered in the evening and late afternoon. Many of the graduate students I knew taught in the city high schools or elementary schools; others worked in publishing; one was in merchandising and wanted to become a teacher; a few had discovered the welfare department, which, among other things, provided jobs for needy scholars and would-be professors. No one could complain about their motives. In good American fashion, they were intent on improving their lot in life. To teach in college offered a more attractive future than teaching in high school or working in welfare.

Not that N.Y.U. actually cared about the needs of

its students. Had it been able to afford a graduate program to which students would be admitted only on a full-time basis, it undoubtedly would have. It had no choice, however.

Just as no one spoke about color at Columbia no one spoke about class at N.Y.U. Very little has been written about the fact that students from working-class or lower-middle-class backgrounds rarely go on to graduate school. There seem to be two basic reasons for this: few scholarships are provided specifically for them, and too few reputable graduate schools encourage part-time study. I cannot think of any Ivy League graduate school, for example, that provides for the student who cannot afford to attend a university full-time. The problem does not attract a great deal of attention, perhaps because the working class has recently managed to attract little but scorn from intellectuals and educators who might have been expected to speak for its interest in the past. No one has high expectations for working-class students; this is why so few of them continue on for the Ph.D. The explanation generally given is that the working-class student is interested in financial rather than in intellectual rewards. Many of them go into elementary or high school teaching; their supposed betters ascribe this to something known as the "civil service mentality," a collective form of limited expectations that the middle-class student apparently sheds from his soul. Or else we are confronted with the argument that they are not as interested in the pure products of intellect and imagination as their middle-class peers are (an argument that, as the academic world itself grows suspicious of intellect and imagination, now works in their favor, but for the most patronizing of reasons).

Ultimately, however, money remains the exploiter. Comparatively few working-class students are able to come up with the money necessary to continue on to a graduate education. Should they choose to take the traditional road of marrying and making the "mistake" of having children, they face an almost insurmountable barrier in their attempt to acquire Ph.D.'s. I do not know of any study of the class backgrounds of American Ph.D.'s over the last three decades, but I believe that such a study would show how few working-class students went on to complete doctorates. How many graduate fellowships are actually reserved for their use or are even available to them? And why is it that so many academicians who plead for understanding of the special situation of blacks and Chicanos and Puerto Ricans simply ignore the white working class? "They have no problems in coming to school," said a liberal colleague to me recently. Tell that to a longshoreman in Brooklyn or a cabbie in the Bronx. "You got to go to college today even to be a goddamn cop" is an expression that is uttered with a terrible sense of frustration. It is difficult not to measure up in America.

I do not wish to make them into something they were not, but I remember my fellow graduate students at N.Y.U. with affection. Their lives did not seem so subordinate to the demands of graduate school, as had the lives of my Furnald Hall peers. Occasionally I confronted a fellow graduate student whose work on his orals preparation or on his doctoral dissertation had made him volubly pathological, but at least N.Y.U. graduate students seemed physically alive, which was more than I felt at Columbia. And we were less competitive with one another. None of us sought to carve out a reputation on the mind of a fellow student. There was neither percentage nor profit in such a venture. At N.Y.U. all rewards were looked upon as fortuitous, accident rather than fate. I needed the fellowship money as much as any of my peers. And need was all that mattered. At Columbia, being selected for anything incurred the antagonism of one's fellows. The reigning intellectualism had so aborted the world that fellowships were regarded as testimony of a person's worth. Rivalries were ferocious. No one could bear the thought of someone else getting a quick leg up on the horse. At N.Y.U. no one took the university or its formal notes of approval seriously enough to stir up jealousy. We knew there was a world outside the university.

What I remember best about Columbia is the feverish inhumanity of the institution itself; what I remember best about the four years I spent at N.Y.U. is the Village. The old apartment buildings on University Place possessed a spirit independent of the university after which the street had been named. No matter how much land N.Y.U. was buying up around the Square, one felt that it would never succeed in incorporating the Village into its own soul. At that time, I could still believe that the school would not press in upon the Village. (It never occurred to me then that the day might come when the Village would press in upon the school.)

It was difficult to think of N.Y.U. as a source of power. The faculty gathered encomiums through its participation in such packaged cereals as *Sunrise Semester*. You could never revere a man who was willing to expose his taped intelligence to the daily 6:30 A.M. audience, to tell them how the Roman empire went into its decline, shook, then collapsed, even when followed by bacon and eggs, coffee, and *Captain Kangaroo*.

How could we take the graduate school seriously? A

library that was best described as a home for runaway boys, kids flocking off the street, out of the cold. Catch forty winks in the drab stalls or the dingy halls. No one thought of the library as a place where he might actually read or study. The chances of finding the book you wanted were poor anyway, although the chances of finding friends were excellent. No one bothered to speak in hushed tones, the traditional form of address at Columbia, since few thought of it as a place for anything other than socializing. At N.Y.U. the library led one away from the mind. The shoddiness was open, the package labeled for all to see. The new and garish student center on the south side of Washington Square was the bait with which N.Y.U. was going to catch its fish. But at least the library was less crowded.

I can virtually call up my year at Columbia at will, so vivid is it in the eye of my own anger. I remember the four years I spent at N.Y.U. with a quiet tolerance and affection. The school never claimed to be any more than it was. At Columbia, present and past fed each other; the university's endowment was its long stretch of history. N.Y.U., on the other hand, possessed ambitions that were greater than its energies. Unable to arouse expectation, it was also unable to disappoint. No one gave it his destiny or sense of worth. Even when it rewarded its students, it remained powerless to affect them greatly.

I think the chief difference between the two schools lay with the faculty. Not only was the quality of teaching better at N.Y.U., but the student here was granted the benefit of his curiosity. Style did not make a student important. Anyone who desired to find out what made the country move was allowed to pursue his quest, however. There were few overseers among the faculty; all my teachers were approachable. For me, the most stimulating experience I had at N.Y.U. was coming into contact with the mind of Henry Bamford Parkes.

He was not the kind of teacher whom undergraduates would select as their favorite professor. Which teacher, dear alumnus, did the most for you during your four years at Holywell College? No, he would not be the recipient of those post-Sputnik great teacher awards that were created in the late fifties in order to make college teaching as popular as quarterbacking. I have been a college teacher now for fourteen years, and I know that students often confuse a teacher's refusal to make demands upon them or his attempt to be someone other than who he is with what they feel is greatness. At the same time, it is nonsense to speak about good teaching as an indefinable quality, a personal magnetism. A good teacher strives to produce a coherent concept of reality; to meet this challenge is to achieve the only substantive victory the profession offers.

Henry Bamford Parkes was not the kind of teacher who would be snapped up today as a charismatic hero. His style is not in vogue. The accusation is not to be handled lightly. He was not dynamic, and in America, especially in the academy, a lack of dynamism is equated with a lack of a sense of mission. As a teacher, he was somewhat shy and retiring. He was not a particularly inspiring lecturer. He did not try to be. He possessed one of those dry English monotones that can exasperate the American ear; it was advisable to arrive at his lectures early and seat yourself in the front if you wanted to hear him. He was not as highly valued by the history department as he should have been, although his colleagues, too, agreed that his was the finest mind in the department. In a world where prestige was measured by publication, he had clearly outdistanced his contemporaries in the department. He created synthesis out of diversity, whereas so many of the other historians at N.Y.U. insisted upon a narrower view of American history. He believed that the teacher of history had to be ready to make distinctions, to discriminate among interpretations. At the same time, he had to bring to his interpretation a willingness to live with complexity.

Henry Bamford Parkes was himself the product of an English education, which had tempered his mind and made him an ideal figure to develop the discipline of American studies at N.Y.U. He had worked in classics and history at Oxford, then emigrated to the United States, where he settled. His continued fascination with this country, I suspect, had a great deal to do with the fact that he was constantly forced to measure it against what his past intellectual experience had been. In 1930, at the age of twenty-six, he joined the faculty at N.Y.U. with a Ph.D. from Michigan. As I write this, he is still teaching at N.Y.U. He has been teaching there for forty years.

I did not meet him until my second year as a graduate student at N.Y.U. He had been on a Fulbright lectureship in Greece. By that time, I had already read *The American Experience*, one of the few books I know that manages to translate the confusion and excitement that American history generates into anything approaching intellectual coherence. In a secondhand bookstore, I tracked down his work on pragmatism as well as his history of Mexico. Here was a historian writing about literature and painting with intelligence and excitement; he did not sound as if he were relieving himself of some painful obligation in explaining the world of culture to the unlettered reader. He wrote as a man who had examined a nation in the process of becoming. It was of inestimable benefit to his students that American life was something for which he felt sympathy, while at the same time he was skeptical of whether it was capable of overcoming its own internal paradoxes.

I remember having dinner with him in the University Restaurant on Eighth Street early in 1968. He had grown more disturbed by the Vietnam War as it went on, and it had forced him, as it had forced so many others, to reexamine the liberalism that he believed was characteristic of American life. He was far too committed an anti-Marxist (he had, in characteristic fashion, gone to the trouble of investigating Marxism in a book published on the eve of the Second World War) to accept the work of younger revisionist historians who simply condemned America as a totality. And yet he was deeply troubled by the war's blatant immorality, by its lack of logic, and by the country's inability to see that while the house was burning down, it was ill-advised to stand outside and water down the garden. For all of his fascination with the country and its history, he never had been able to make up his mind about what it represented to him. He assumed its uniqueness. He admitted its singularity. Whether or not this pleased him remained a mystery.

The same qualities that made him an effective teacher made him an effective historian. His classical studies at Oxford had given him an idea of what the word *civili-*

zation meant. He would not indulge in intellectual chauvinism, for while he saw the country's uniqueness, he saw it, too, as part of the general movement of Western civilization. He warned us against seeing American life as so singular that it would avoid classification, just as he warned us against looking at it as a mere mirror image of European civilization. He brought to his classes his own search for the larger whole and never permitted students to look at the development of this country in isolation. Cultures were not created fully formed; they evolved slowly, sometimes with great difficulty.

He seems to me that rarest of teachers, an individual whose ideas actually matched the quality of his mind. He did not expect his students to succumb to his personality or to dissect his psyche or to analyze his mannerisms. He expected them to respond only to his ideas and to the genuine confusion so many of us share over the formation and development of America. He liked his students, partly because he was a shy but sociable human being, partly because they served as proof of a certain intellectual continuity that belongs to civilization itself. During the time that I was at N.Y.U., he built up a following among graduate students in American studies and in history that genuinely surprised and pleased him. We all thought of him as our mentor, regardless of which professor we were doing our dissertations with. In the years to come, when we met at conventions or at social gatherings, we would invariably discuss Henry Bamford Parkes. It annoyed us that his work had not had a better reception from his fellow historians. We attributed it to the facile cultural ignorance of many American historians. We were annoyed and puzzled and sometimes angry. I suspect that deep down, however, we never expected anything else. In the academic world, reputations were commodities that could be bought and sold. And while I enjoyed my graduate studies at N.Y.U., I recognized the school's commercial orientation. There had been no display stalls to illustrate the art of selling at Oxford. If it was a deficiency, it was more than welcome in Professor Parkes.

Chapter Four

By April, 1960, my doctoral dissertation had been completed, accepted by my advisers, and was waiting to be bound along with the thousands of other doctoral dissertations that had been completed in America that year. To all intents and purposes, my life as a student had ended. Whatever I may have felt about that life, I was left with little time for sentimental reflection. I was one more young Ph.D. looking for a job, and that was enough to make anyone question the fates that had sent him into college teaching.

I thought I had few illusions remaining about the academic world, but I was not really prepared for the M.L.A. convention. It was probably like every other M.L.A. convention held since that organization chose to abandon its scholarly character in favor of serving the profession as an employment agency. And the Statler-Hilton had played host to any number of similar functions—brassiere buyers, photography-equipment salesmen, knitted-goods manufacturers, professional football drafts. Only at the M.L.A., the bidding was for mind rather than for meat and muscle or lady's lingerie. And there were slightly different rules and mores to be observed. Department chairmen walked around with minds soothed by alcohol but bolstered by the power to hire. How did *they* weigh the value of Ph.D.'s on this market? Was there a point system, a sliding scale pegged to the school at which you had done your doctorate? So much poundage for Yale and Harvard and Berkeley, that perpetual *ménage à trois* that the vast majority of graduate students looked on with the covetous eyes of the outcast. And beneath that on the scale? Who could say what came next? How much for Princeton? How much for Hopkins? How much for N.Y.U.? How much for those blistered southern citadels of a truer intellectualism than most northerners were willing to admit, Duke and North Carolina universities, still trapped by the peculiar provincialism that had long reigned in academia, the prejudice against the southern that moored the white lightning of minds to the nebulous gravel of academic reputation? "These shits are going to kill me yet," I heard one soft southern voice whisper to the unresponsive roof of the Statler-Hilton bar. They had burned him for his credentials.

The hotel smell was musty and damp, the smell of a New York winter. Thick carpeting, feet moving from room to room, being caught in the elevator with dense throngs of deodorized but sweating people, all of us nervous, all panting for that single interview that could be carried off with the meticulous lucidity of our fantasies. And the halls peppered with the shouts of the wives of department chairmen greeting each other, smiling in their reflected pools of power. And the conversations in the bar. Is it possible to carry the humanistic vision away from this scene intact? Three hysterical, obviously exhausted graduate students meeting over drinks in the bar of the Statler-Hilton, arguing, gesticulating in the damp heated air. And about what? About which of their schools possessed the better eighteenth-century man! Here was the prestige of accomplishment, the runoff of ambition. They could have been comparing three quarterbacks.

In the lobby I spotted Professor Parkes, who had just walked in. "Depressing, isn't it?" I nodded, relieved to be able to speak to someone I knew without having to mold my face, to smile, to pretend that the scene around me did not violate every reason I could think of for having chosen to enter this profession. Parkes steered me to the bar and bought me a drink. It was obvious that I didn't want to talk about the convention, and so he began to tell me about the time he had spent in Mexico. In five minutes I was oblivious to the surroundings. For the moment ambition was pared from the soul like layers from an onion.

Only for the moment, though, because soon the battle began again. I went dutifully to the next appointment and watched as the chairman interviewing me gazed at his watch, anticipating the next arrival. And while my mouth maintained its fixed smile, I fantasized his doom in the fetid swamp of the M.L.A. hiring hall. I wanted to believe he fed off the shredded egos of his graduate students. It was more probable that he was simply a decent, hard-working, confused man who had not known that being a department chairman would be quite like this. Meanwhile, both of us were left to struggle for dignity. Why didn't he just turn to me and ask, "Who needs this?" Then again, he probably would have been just as grateful to have heard something similar from me. Instead, we both continued to play at being proper academics. Were we too sensitive to notice the atmosphere in these hotel corridors, that borderline country in which man in the mass fights off all his instincts? No. The walls of the ivory tower had long since been razed to the ground. How much reality could we surrender to pretense?

I should have stayed away from conventions. I didn't want to go to California, to join the state college system and lie on the sun-drenched campuses. "I swim, I teach the young pretties, I lie on the beach, and I dream," said my friend and former graduate school colleague at N.Y.U. as he clasped my hand and pointed me in the direction of the bar. "Life is simple. Literature is still loved; just a more distant mistress now. The most immediate problem I face is how much insurance to take out on my house this year. Even the Dodgers have moved, friend." I asked about the book he had wanted to write: the definitive study of American prose styles. He himself had called it that. "Never mind about the book," he said when I questioned him. The edge of ambition could be blunted, I reminded him. "Kriegel, no matter how much you read, you will always remain a city child. Learn! The world will not miss your studies of the true and beautiful." I protested. I had my doubts. "Kriegel," he shrugged, "you are helpless. As a reclamation project, you are out of my element. California is another world."

Which was my out, I now understood. For I did not really want to leave New York. New York, I insisted, was a prototype for what might yet be accomplished throughout the country. The less possible teaching in New York became, the more attractive it grew for me, if for no other reason than that students here were classified by their ignorance and were, in a strange way, dependent on their yearning for knowledge of the familiar. How else could they outwit the world? And what would I do in California? The dream of oranges and blonde co-eds vanished. My friend was right. I was out of his element.

It now seemed terribly important to remain in New York. Not that I was under any illusions about how bright New York students were. Behind the sophomoric romanticism with which I justified my decision to remain in New York lay the reality of the naked desperation of the New York student who had retained the primitive desire to see things fall into place. "Do not shit me," is the chief request he makes. Good enough. And difficult enough, too. He was challenge for any teacher. The prospects of teaching in the city were filled with rewards and pitfalls that I would not have encountered in California. The New York student did not yet possess any real sophistication. He did have the advantage of being able to call upon a range of experience that was both narrower and more intense than that of his out-of-city cousin. The most brutalized adolescent in New York is aware of what is due him and of how his own potential has been distorted. Like most Americans, he will accept the idea that the country is his for the taking. At the same time, he remains frightened of the energy and output demanded of him.

Everything, he has been taught, has its price. And if he is to storm the fortress, then is it unreasonable to ask what treasure lies behind the walls?

If remaining in New York was to be an attempt to come to terms with myself, I think it proved worthwhile. I felt that I would only be throwing my anger away on the rest of the world; in New York it might show a profit for both me and my students. To work with what you know, using your own past, is to be faced with the kind of opportunity that occurs so infrequently it cannot be rejected out of hand. Undoubtedly my New York provincialism. Provincialism could be strangely functional, though. The blonde co-eds might be pinions for the ego. The California sun might warm the body. Yet the stringent acerbity bred in the student's bone by the very failure of high school education in this city— where else could I encounter that?

My decision to remain in New York did not assure my getting a job there. New York might be a beacon for me, but I was not the only one aware of its attractions; it was a veritable magnet for other fledgling Ph.D's. Other than Columbia, which I still hated vehemently (and Columbia would never have hired a recent N.Y.U. Ph.D.), and Hunter, where I sensed my role would have to be that of the returning prodigal, I think I applied to every college, community college, and university in the city. By mid-March I had received an offer of an assistant professorship in the English department of Long Island University. City College also made me an offer, which arrived after I had already accepted the L.I.U. position. Even though it was only mid-April, I felt that it would not be ethical to accept the City offer, which was renewed the following winter. When the second offer came, I no longer worried about the ethics of my decision.

L.I.U., I soon discovered, was marked by sharp incongruities: on one hand, a board of trustees that was a Marxist caricature of an American university's board of trustees, bloated with bankers and real estate operators and an assortment of *arriviste* fat cats, the servants of millionaires who had themselves become millionaires; on the other, an English department chairman who was still waging the Trotskyite-Stalinist war, who excoriated McCarthyism but sent a young instructor packing without even giving him the ostensible reasons for his dismissal. This man dutifully herded his department together when the government ordered air raid drills and was amazed to discover that some of us resisted. There was a lack of balance about L.I.U., a sense of definition that had gone astray somewhere along the line. The incongruities of the place infected me, too. I spent hour after hour cursing the fates that had sent me here and resolved to quit teaching if I were unable to leave the school within three years.

Yet it was at L.I.U. that I first really began to woo my profession, to bend my knee before the vision of educational possibility. The contradictions that I feel about teaching today began during that year at L.I.U. There were moments then when I believed that teaching was as fine a vocation as a man could claim; there were other moments, not as frequent but no less intense, when I cursed the pretense and pomposity of academic life and wondered aloud why I hadn't chosen to be a lawyer or architect. Teaching was the center of my L.I.U. experience. I had, of course, taught during two of my years as a graduate student at N.Y.U. My focus there, however, had never really been on the classroom; it couldn't have been. I was a graduate student, and a graduate student had certain obligations. I had been a dutiful, conscientious teacher. My primary object, though, had been the acquisition of my doctorate. I had, strangely enough, rarely thought very much about teaching; I just did it. And while I was certainly aware of my students and even responsive to them and to their needs, they were not the chief object of my attention. At Long Island University, the students were central. They simply fell into one's life. They were there for the claiming, for no one had ever told them how interesting they were, no one had ever treated them as anything other than marionettes to be jerked and hustled for budgets and regents examinations. Unfashionable children: blue-collar Jewish students who had not been suckled on rich mammaries; Italians who had long since been convinced that alternatives were simple and inevitable, either drift with the neighborhood gangs or edge your way to respectability with the civil service; Brooklyn Swedes and Irish Catholic nursing students and Greeks from places in New York I did not know and even a few out-of-town students, all of them conned into the acceptance of failure. They were not bright enough to make it elsewhere. They were there for the claiming, and after the first week, when I came to know a few of them, I was amazed that so few of my colleagues felt that they were worth claiming. These students taught me that teaching is as important as I had believed it to be at Hunter; they made it an act of dedication.

What they really needed, it occurs to me now, was a faculty eager to embrace the very lack of academic respectability L.I.U. offered. Instead, their faculty comprised teachers who were still bitter about not having been granted tenure at Brooklyn College and teachers who had been working for their doctorates for so long that their energy had dissipated and they merely accepted the task in front of them. They were teachers who were reputed to be inadequate in one way or another. This faculty had been punished. Unfortunately, it chose to get even by using what talent it possessed to try to make L.I.U. a better institution, when what it should have been doing was using what was there. Conversation in the faculty dining room, when it was not about salaries or about the chances of acquiring medical benefits, was about standards. This was the first time I heard teachers talk a great deal about standards, but I soon learned that at L.I.U., at City, at Harvard, at Oshkosh State Teachers College, faculty inevitably talk about standards. At L.I.U. the question of the moment was whether or not approval from the Middle States Association of Colleges and Secondary Schools would be maintained. The school was seeking respectability and the Middle States Association bestowed the gift on those whom it viewed with favor. If the school maintained its approval, it would be *better*. *Good, better, best*. The bases for approval were not altogether to my liking, for the association's idea of what constituted a college was not necessarily my own. I believed that the responsibility of the urban university was to teach man in his cities, but I suspect that the association looked upon urbanism as rather parochial, something that the college should get away from. The faculty looked forward to the out-of-town students who might apply to L.I.U. once Middle States' approval had been reaffirmed. Had I told my colleagues that they already possessed the students they wanted, I suspect they would have been amazed. Students were a statistical compilation—numbers, objects, chess pieces, badges for consumption by

press and radio and the bureau of statistics. I suppose
I shouldn't blame the faculty or even the administration.
Like the students, they thought of the college as a
dumping ground. It would take more than approval by
the Middle States Association to convince them of their
respectability.

L.I.U. ground its faculty down as it ground its students
down. It ignored the potential of both. It insisted on
dedication and commitment and then it pulled the rug
out from underneath anyone who was dedicated or
committed. It pretended to be a part of urban America,
while its board of trustees plotted expansion into the
suburbs. The school didn't realize its own assets; it
ignored the legitimate appeal it could make. It was a
school populated by those who had not made it elsewhere, the educational "failures" of New York's working
and lower-middle classes, and it was ashamed of its
constituency. It wished to make gentlemen of them all.
And the price demanded: a silent acceptance of the
official incongruities—admirals running colleges, real
estate operators ruling the world of intellect, former
Trotskyites who wrote books about religion in Shakespeare. Where else but in New York?

Inevitably one begins with the setting. It was peculiarly
urban, even more so than N.Y.U. or Columbia, and it
chipped away at your affections. It was much smaller
and much poorer than either of the others, and it was
completely absorbed by downtown Brooklyn. The
physical plant was situated on a postage-stamp-sized mod-
ernistic "campus" named after the real estate operator
who overseered its board and was dominated by a con-
ventionally ugly dormitory building that looked like a

squared-off beehive. The student at L.I.U. was framed
by the harsh lights and dead ends of downtown Brooklyn, a forlorn and cancerous region, stuck like a city
blight between Ft. Greene and Brooklyn Heights and
the Grand Army Plaza. What is there about that part
of Brooklyn that suggests a man struck down while
holding a winning lottery ticket in his hand? How
strange to call the school Long Island University when
it was stuck among old factories and gas stations. This
was the setting of the Brooklyn Center of Long Island
University. Well, the setting could be ignored, at least by
the trustees, whose eyes were on the C. W. Post campus on
the Island. A Zeckendorf was not a Rockefeller; he himself was a mere servant to the true vaults of wealth. Be
advised that he had not spent all his time waiting in the
wings to head a school for drop-outs. No, he had nailed
his name to this university. A patch of concrete called
a campus, a dormitory building, plans for a library never
completed, gates donated by an alumni association not
yet successful enough to warrant real attention from
the world. The eyes of L.I.U.'s trustees turned elsewhere. Long Island was something else; Long Island
demanded. Whatever the urban stepchild was given, he
was given with a reluctant charity, the pitch of pennies
against concrete. And so the proposed library building
turned into a shoddy, meretricious classroom building.
"Never mind," a colleague said. "What would these kids
want with a library?" What was the school's constituency? Not, apparently, the students. Not, at least,
unless they had been dipped in the fat of the trustees'
rhetoric and then burned to a harmless crisp.

Street lights dissect the water-slick creosote of Flatbush Avenue Extension and turn it into a surrealist fan-

tasy. This is the way memories of the school came back to me: embedded in neon urbanism, garish, the Paramount Theater marquee still blinking its message into the wet Brooklyn air, rivaled by the huge neon sign across the street that topped the domed Brooklyn Dime Savings Bank. While I was teaching, the Paramount closed its doors and was converted into a school auditorium, stripped of its old life by television and educational progress both; this was one of the few stories about L.I.U. that appeared in the *Times*. All those signs: "Be Sure It's Hebrew National," "Texaco," "Bartons," "Howard Clothes," the restaurant across the street, Junior's, that was one of the distinct advantages of teaching there. And the smells that had drifted over from the Lower East Side years ago. The sour smell of the streets and all the open-windowed stores that sold knishes and pizza and franks, spice to the expectation of Junior's pickles. In such an atmosphere were the students trained to an ersatz propriety. They would yet be taught to ignore all their senses; they would learn to transform themselves, to make themselves conscious of "new opportunities." In the words of the great real estate operator, they were "an urban student body drawn from middle- and lower-income families." From the administration, from the faculty, from one another, they would accept instruction in order to change their inner beings. The money, however, was fed into the C. W. Post College.

There is little that I can say to romanticize the students. And yet not even at City was I more aware of the unique qualities that students bring to a classroom. More, perhaps, than any others I have known, they suffered from the American instinct for competitiveness, the desire to prove that the self is worthy of the nation. Rating systems, grades, obligations to improve, the requirements of the Middle States Association, these had beset them all their lives. The best of them were misfits, and they knew it. The Brooklyn-born student who had dropped out of Harpur College because, although he had come through his freshman year with a straight-A average, he had not touched his saxophone. "It was too much of a price. Once I just wanted to play jazz. They had me so that I was going like a machine and thinking that it was human." The Greek from a school for bright high school students in Ohio who had simply packed in Antioch at the end of his second year because, as he said, "I want to see where F. Scott Fitzgerald made it." Or the son of the Astoria butcher who insisted that I read his girl friend's poetry, which, he assured me, was going "to flatten the literary world on its ass." They had few expectations from their educations and few expectations from the world. They had no real idea of what was getting them down, and they would have dismissed the idea that they could make demands as absurd. Unfortunately, they accepted too many American myths without question. They believed that their parents lived off the fat of the land, when their fathers, in reality, drove laundry trucks or sliced meat in supermarkets or waited on tables. They had few images from their own lives on which to focus, and so they sought salvation from progressive jazz, the purest product of black America, or from F. Scott Fitzgerald, the most rugged of American individualists, or from T. S. Eliot, who would have viewed their Brooklyn with a mixture of bewilderment and contempt.

They were all different, although most of them felt that they were part of a group. In the seventies they would actually have stood with middle America, though none of them had yet heard the term. The first one I usually think of is George. He came from Astoria, and he had raised himself ever since the age of thirteen. An excellent student of literature, he retreated before any-one's praise. Life had taught him caution: to settle for less rather than to bid for more. He was at L.I.U. be-cause he had mistakenly assumed that his high school average was not good enough to "make Queens." George expected little from his life; he could not trust the legitimacy of his own imagination because no one had ever told him before that his title was as good as that of the next man. When I told him, he did not believe me. George was one of those I was determined to reclaim. I suspect that I somehow wanted to fashion him after my own image. Maybe I was trying to lift the common heritage off both our shoulders.

He was suspicious of America, suspicious of every-thing. He lacked all sense of the ethnic. In 1960 anything ethnic was unfashionable, and if anyone had suggested to George that he was the heir of Dante and Pico della Mirandola, he would have laughed. He accepted the existence of the *mafioso* in his neighborhood as he ac-cepted the existence of General Motors, with neither admiration nor scorn. A living was a living. "My old man thought it was a big thing to be Italian," he once told me. "He used to call himself an Italian-American. Jesus, you know when he got to Italy. During the war. He saw Anzio. Then he got wounded. Lost a finger. And the dumb bastard, he told me that his finger was part of the Italian landscape. His Italian finger, he called it."

He had no sense of class either. Having been born in Astoria he had an almost built-in hostility toward those who made a great deal of money. But when I tried to talk to him about literature in terms of class, he dismissed what I had to say with a wave of his hand. One day he entered my office to introduce me to his girl. "I want you to meet Marge," he said, bringing her into the office. She was a pretty, dark-haired girl with an Irish name. It was a natural enough gesture for George. The professor thought he was smart; therefore, he was going to show the professor exactly how smart he was. George made his point. He was going to marry Marge, get a job teaching in junior high school or high school. He was not going on to graduate school, he was not going to be a college teacher. That took too long. He was not going to be a writer. A writer was a social bandit and George had taken from Astoria, along with an expectation of failure, a desire for respectability. Were he ever to visit Paris, it would be as a tourist, with the pretty, dark-haired Irish girl at his side.

George was like so many of the students I liked at L.I.U. They filled me with anger and pride. Blue collar, intelligent, sensitive, distant, playing tough, afflicted with the great American disease, the conviction that they could not measure up. They were frugal when they spent their energies, convinced that *they* were lacking, not the country. Settle for less: that was their unspoken motto. Their American dream. Their reality.

Not many teachers filled with missionary zeal were attracted to L.I.U. Those few who were got out as soon as they could. For the students who cluttered the concrete patches of the Zeckendorf campus were obviously not those who inspired dreams of vital and meaningful change in the university. They were hemmed in by the very mundane truths that their teachers were seeking to escape. The daughters of the rich had been rubbed by the sweet mystery of distance, and the sons of black steelworkers were bathed in the pungent waters of revolutionary rhetoric. Lady Bountiful and Bottom Dog—it was a strange but essentially American combination. Meanwhile, students like George gravitated toward schools such as L.I.U., working for certification to teach in junior high school or high school; they still dreamed of Fitzgerald diving into the fountain at the Plaza with his clothes on. Here, then, was America.

My classes at L.I.U. gave me the feeling that I was the first man in the world to try his hand at teaching. They were outrageous, filled with sudden illuminations that had nothing to do with what I had thought constituted teaching and were certainly very different from the classes I had taught at N.Y.U. At Commerce I had found an excessive respect for the products of mind; at the Square, a belief that there were certain regular niches to which the student accommodated himself. L.I.U., though, made teaching an almost prophetic experience. A good class, a response from the students, and I would drive home from Flatbush Avenue in a state of quiet euphoria. Never was teaching to drain me as it did at L.I.U.; never, perhaps, was it to reward me in quite this way either. I soon reached an absolute nadir of expectation, and so anything a class of mine accomplished was a strange, personal triumph. During my second term there, I taught an advanced course in poetry. Most of the students were older men and women who were working and whose reasons for going to college at night were varied. The way in which they drove themselves awed me; at ten in the evening they were still fresh, still ready for another bout with the passion of Blake or the crisp subtleties of Donne. For a class of English majors, they were not particularly skilled writers. Yet they managed to convey their enthusiasm. And I would arrive home at eleven in the evening, buoyed by their enthusiasm, their sense of privilege in having encountered the pure product of the imagination itself.

The school itself, however, was simply too much to take. Neither rebel nor conformist, it dreamed of being both. Students seemed constantly pressured and harassed, denied their basic right to define the world for themselves. So many forces existed to tell them what they did and did not know. They had been programmed to accept their difficulties, conditioned to think of themselves as unintellectual, incapable. Psychologically they had little to fall back on. They lacked a belief in the reality of their bodies or nature or sports or some aspect of living that might have indicated some viable possibilities of existence for them. They were not capable of viewing themselves as exotics as they might have in the thirties, but then they knew nothing about that decade.

And they descended on such schools as L.I.U., St. Francis, Hofstra, Adelphi, or a thousand and one similar institutions that dot the educational landscape, on guard against what might await them. Their teachers, for the most part, shared their skepticism. Teaching at such parochial places was not particularly rewarding, nor did it give one status among liberals in the profession. Educating blacks could always be looked at as revolutionary, despite one's frequent suspicions that one's black students were more often than not rhetoricians of the revolution and soul brothers of the middle class. There was little glamour, however, in educating the sons and daughters of brick layers and construction workers —those bastions of middle-class paranoia. That was simply busy work.

What saved that year for me was the reality of the classroom. Never mind the students' conviction that they were uneducable. The sophomore class with which I worked on *The Heart of Darkness* told me the opposite. I could not teach students to pull the reality of literature out of themselves; I could only illustrate for them how it was done, and, if I was lucky, I could watch the ideas begin to penetrate. Gradually reading had ceased to be a chore; it had been transformed into an important act. Where before they had been most aware of their own inarticulateness, my students now began to discover the power of language. At first, thinking about literature was important only because it was thinking. Then it became thinking about books, about plays. They did not have to justify what they were doing. Just to do it well afforded them a certain pleasure. And to be interested in doing it again afforded happiness. It was very easy to commit oneself to these students, and learning that was my greatest success.

One of my classes was filled with would-be nurses. The Brooklyn Center had recently begun a joint program with a Brooklyn hospital to combine a B.S. with training in nursing. The program was one more manifestation of the American need for certification and degrees, and yet I really enjoyed teaching these students. The idea was not so much to teach them as to chip away at their past so that they might come to terms with the demands of higher education. The great majority of them were graduates of one or another Catholic high school for girls. Although they were terribly frightened of books, they were also filled with an excessive respect for the demands of the mind. They made the world of art and ideas completely unreal, a form of totemism both sensually "dirty" and frightfully "liberating." I cannot think of students who uttered the word *professor* in quite the same way as these students did, with an angular breathlessness that made me suspect it was a momentary substitute for *father*. "Father, I have sinned. . . ." They read *Hamlet* with a parochial school mentality that insisted that sin was inevitable, punishment deserved. The process used to arrive at that homily did prove intriguing for them, though. If they did not bring to their reading a depth of critical penetration, they brought to it an identifiable sense of what was and what was not right. "Sin or not," said one little girl with a drawn, pinched face, "I think he should have stabbed him while he prayed." Perhaps it was too narrow a view of Hamlet, but it said a great deal about her, about the way in which the educational chipping might have been working in her life. She knew what it was not to measure up. Horizons were limited in her world. Just to have moved, in the space of one short term, from thinking of reading as sacrilegious and illicit was a marked advance in her own battle to claim a personality. Once shown the world as something offered her rather than something intended to put her in her place, she became deeply excited.

At the end of the term, a number of girls approached my desk. One of them, who blushed a great deal in class, acted as spokesman, while the rest remained a few feet away. "We just want to tell you," she said hesitantly, "how much we appreciate your having worked with us." I hadn't done anything special, I insisted. I had done nothing that I did not do in my other classes. "That's just it," she continued. "That's why we want to thank you. Because you didn't do anything different." There it was before me, the legacy of class.

I left L.I.U., as I knew I would once the offer of a job at City was renewed that February. I'm happy that I left when I did, for leaving later would have been more difficult. L.I.U. had seemed a floundering institution from the beginning, a school at which no discernible purpose had yet emerged except for the need to survive. Teaching there had been extremely rewarding; being there had been extremely disheartening. The drop in rank when I went to City—I would move down from assistant professor to instructor—was more than compensated for by a healthy increase in salary. I had no illusions about what I was doing. I was getting out while the getting was good.

It was, however, a decision that left me with a far greater sense of loss than I expected. I had grown to like the students very much during the year, but I sensed that they needed the kind of commitment that would have drained me and possibly even destroyed the very joy I took in teaching. While I met a number of dedicated teachers at L.I.U., those who had been at the school for more than six or seven years seemed completely burned out, as if the need to do the job had left them hollow. I had to get out. There had been too many conversations in Junior's with full professors whose sense of purpose had been stripped away. In spite of the students, who had rewarded me by working far beyond my expectations and by enjoying their work, I could not justify remaining there. Outside the windows of the Paramount Theater building, Brooklyn was dying, choking, a touch of cancer in the throat, its nerves rubbed raw, its citizens fleeing. It no longer offered even the dream of resurrection. L.I.U., I assumed, would die even before Brooklyn.

The students had been the only part of the university's life that I had enjoyed. They brought home everything I believed about the need for literacy, the benefits of education. As a group, they had less money and less independence than students at N.Y.U.; they certainly lacked the talent that I was to find among my students at City; and they did not seem even to occupy the same planet as the undergraduates I had observed at Columbia. They produced few prize winners, few students who would leave their mark on the important graduate schools in the nation. But they possessed, as a group, a remarkable kind of honesty, and they asked little of their teachers other than a pledge of faith and a certain amount of patience. No one ever thought of them as one of the redemptive aspects of American higher education, although, of course, they were. They were better people than anyone had given them reason to believe. And they deserved better than what they had received, either from their teachers or from the society that regarded them as men and women of little worth and left them imprisoned in their sense of worthlessness.

Chapter Five

Long before I began to teach at the City College of New York, it had come to represent for me, as it did for most of the friends with whom I grew up, the best that man in his cities could expect in the way of a college education. The very name spoke of our urbanism, mingling the identity of New York's students with the changeable values of city life. Even after Brooklyn College, Queens College, and Hunter College had been founded, City remained the prototype of the "subway school." Perhaps it is because of this that the school lends itself to extremes of feeling; its alumni either encase it in loving romanticism or else surrender to the popular image of an American university and curse City for its inability to provide a traditional college atmosphere. City imposed its own presence; the smell of the subways, the shoving elbows in the packed trains were ever-present even in the neo-Gothic Shephard Hall.

From the moment that I began teaching there, I sensed that I would love it. And yet I must have known on that very first day that there would be moments when I would hate the college and pray for its obliteration. It demanded so much of the teacher; it demanded even more of the student. When I began teaching there, City College typified New York, even in its dilemmas. It still does. More, perhaps, than any other urban university in this country, it is part of the surrounding landscape. Unlike Columbia, City never existed outside the boundaries of the neighborhood, even when City had so few black students that the residents of those Harlem streets could not help but angrily look at it as a white man's island in a black sea. More than Hunter, Brooklyn, or Queens, it had probably remained closest to the ideals of a municipal college, for its chief function, when I arrived in September, 1961, was still the education of the children of New York's working and lower-middle classes. City, of course, could no longer be thought of as a proletarian Harvard; the time when it had been filled with the sons of sweatshop workers and pushcart peddlers had long since passed. Organized labor had achieved better lives for New York's workers; as a consequence, the working class appeal of the college had lessened. When I came to City, it still served its urban constituency, but the fathers of my students were more likely to be unionized plumbers or electricians than piece workers in the garment industry. And yet there was no doubt in my mind, as there was no doubt in the minds of its alumni, that City was essentially different from other colleges. The very embodiment of the urban university beset by the problems of men in their cities, this college still reminded its students of the possibilities that life held for them. The record of the college in the past remained proof that one could join the ranks of society and yet maintain a certain core of self intact. Although the madness of urban man often looked threatening and all-engulfing, it was still possible to work steadily and sanely, quietly educating oneself and managing to fulfill a meaningful function—doctor, lawyer, teacher, engineer.

City had always been a school at which the students rather than the faculty created the tone. It had achieved a reputation for academic excellence, a reputation built by the aggressive intellectualism of its students rather than on the record of its faculty. Even when the faculty pointed with justifiable pride to such luminaries in its midst as Morris Raphael Cohen, even when it dutifully recited the names of those literary critics and physicists and historians who had evolved within its bosom and returned to teach at the college, it was the students who carried on the reputation of City College. There were a number of distinguished scholars at City when I arrived, including the chairman of my own department. Yet I never met a student who had chosen to attend City College because of the reputation of its faculty.

Students were not considered any more important here than they were at other schools; they certainly did not demand the rights and privileges of adults. The bureaucracy at City was predictable, wholly representative of urban man, and it performed with passionate inefficiency. The first registration I witnessed at City was a carbon copy of the ordeal I had faced at Hunter. "This place is like a goddamn hospital," said a freshman to me that very first week. "They're always taking your temperature." It was easy enough to see what he meant.

Even though they were treated like children, the students bestowed their prestige on the college. And it was the students, not the faculty, to whom the young teacher automatically gravitated; it was the students, not the faculty, who seemed, even in 1961, most receptive to ideas, most willing to cut through to the deeper levels of their own awareness. The students annually captured more than their share of Woodrow Wilson fellowships, and they descended in droves on the best graduate schools in the country. They were aware of the college's reputation and of the fact that they had created it. In a sense, they were closer to the faculty than students at any other college I know of; at the same time, even before the school became again politicized in the mid-sixties, there had been a subtle reversal of relationships. The brighter students simply assumed that whatever worth and prestige the college possessed emanated from them and from the legacy of City's alumni. The faculty was more or less tolerated.

The City College of New York was founded in 1847, brought to birth with a referendum as its midwife. As president of the board of education, Townsend Harris had placed his proposal to establish a free academy before the people of New York City, and the good burghers had voted overwhelmingly, 19,305 to 3,409, to make Townsend Harris' democratic dream a reality; they created a college in which the rich and the poor could rub shoulders. City's urban character immediately manifested itself. The poor quickly discovered that, more often than not, they were jostling only each other's shoulders. Even in the nineteenth century, I assume, the City student was struggling to fight off the world and was desperately anxious to succeed. The college was, from the first, part of one of the most significant of all American experiments, the democratization of higher education. And history does repeat itself. The arguments opposed to the school's founding foreshadow the arguments that raged about the policy of open admissions, instituted in 1970. From the beginning, there was a battle between those who felt the world of culture and education embraced only the interests of the "better people" and those who welcomed the college as an intellectual and economic leveler; in 1847, the "better people" tried to barricade themselves against a "pauper class" whom they feared would prey upon the "active, industrious and affluent portion of the community." Townsend Harris was a man of great vision, a responsible merchant prince, a future diplomat, an important citizen of a young and aggressive country. I suspect that the college was his way of taking revenge upon New York for what it had denied him. Had he been born thirty years later, he might have been the very prototype of Horatio Alger, and yet there must have been moments when his own lack of a college education rankled. It was to his credit and to the credit of the citizens of New York that the college was permitted to set up a liberal admissions policy; the school was to be supported out of public tax funds and students were to be selected on the basis of ability alone. It remains a monumental step in the history of higher education in America, the first time that the people of an American city had created a free public institution of higher learning through the ballot. "Open the doors to all," cried Townsend Harris. "Let the children of the rich and the poor take their seats together and know of no distinction save that of industry, good conduct, and intellect." If that proclamation seems less than revolutionary today, its vision still offers itself for the taking. Some may feel it offers itself for the scoffing.

The City College of New York maintains its appeal because, whatever its failings, it continues to serve a constituency that is unlike any other in the nation, one with a desperate need for education. Not even the state universities established under the Morrill Land Grant Act of 1862 have maintained the kind of theoretical allegiance to democratic education that City has. The school demanded scholastic ability; in return, it showed students a way into the larger society. I still find Townsend Harris' vision appealing, even when I bitterly despair of the culture itself, ranking it out with all the egalitarian venom I can muster. Who wants to join such a society? I would ask myself time and again. Of what value was a free college education when it forced you to accommodate a country that squandered your potential on the money-making ventures of American life?

That was no more than the bitter rinds of the fruit, however. City's uniqueness had to be acknowledged. As a college, it did not so much educate as translate, bridging worlds not necessarily meant to be bridged. The very fact that it had done this successfully made the college's bland acceptance of some of New York's harsh realities all the more infuriating. There was, as evidence of City's success, the long list of distinguished alumni—Lewis Mumford and Felix Frankfurter, Jonas Salk and Ernest Nagel, George Washington Goethals and Arthur Kornberg.

City gives to its students. No doubt it did the same in 1847. And the greatest gift it offers to them is one another. They have been formed in the crucible of an educational system that teaches them to depend upon themselves and upon one another. Their teachers might prefer alternatives to the kind of student City produces, but the school's successful alumni are usually content, always harking back to what the school was like during their own undergraduate days.

Perhaps the students' dependence upon one another is simply a reflection of City's role within the larger society. For the college had not gained its own distinctive style until the arrival of Eastern European Jewish immigrants in New York toward the end of the nineteenth and beginning of the twentieth centuries. The college placed its stamp on the sons of these immigrants, but there can be little doubt that the immigrant children placed their stamp on the college, too. They used their intellectual entrepreneurship as a form of primal energy; they removed ideas from the realm of polite discussion and gave to them a currency with which one might purchase a reputation in America and drive a stake into the witch's heart of success. Because the college was free, it was the one that the children of immigrants usually attended, and this probably occasioned the deep sentimental attachment of many alumni. City was the portal to the promised land. One meets a lawyer in Larchmont, a motion picture producer in California, an engineer in Seattle, a chemist in Florida, a doctor in Chicago for whom a City College diploma has become visible proof of American claims. The legacy of the school bred its own provincialism, in part because it offered such extremes to the imagination. How many other public colleges in America are geared to making the WASP a stranger in his own land? City simply reversed, if only on the surface, the roles of insider and outsider. During

what came to be known as the school's "salad days," the
1930s, the typical City undergraduate must have been
deeply confused about his place in America. He might
claim the nation as his by the prerogatives of intellect
and imagination, but he *belonged* only to New York.

I think of my life as a teacher at City College in three
distinct periods. From 1961 to 1964, I was an instructor
whose primary task was to teach required courses to
freshmen and sophomores. In 1964, I left the college
for a year abroad. In June, 1965, I returned as a tenured
assistant professor, only to discover that both the college
and I had been swept up in the political whirlwinds that
were beginning to stir in academia. I taught for three
more years before I left for another year abroad. In
September, 1969, I returned to a battered and bruised
college licking its wounds and seeking a new justification
for its existence. I tend to think of that first period of my
life at City in terms of my students, of the second in
terms of how politics enmeshed both students and faculty, and of the third in terms of my own growing confusion about the problems confronting urban universities
in this country.

The students during those first three years still possessed characteristics similar to my own when I had
been an undergraduate at Hunter. In 1961 they still had
a defined sense of purpose, although purpose evaporated
in many of the best of them soon after they graduated.
If school was not their problem, the outside world soon
proved to be. Yet they were able to distinguish between
what was taking place at the college and what was taking
place in the outside world. However, by 1967 the dis-

tinction had blurred for many of them. Not only did the college reflect the world outside its gates, it frequently overwhelmed that world, and so, to a politicized student body, what occurred within City College's gates had an intensity all its own. The political life of a student became his overwhelming concern. When I first began teaching there, the college was still clinging to its heritage; it was still fervently intellectual. The student who belonged, intellectually and emotionally, to the thirties could be found at City, but he was an anachronism. He seemed to have fallen out of time if not out of place as he moved across the campus formulating the revolution that had not yet come.

Phil was such a student. He was a swarthy, muscular, dark-haired Jew from the Bronx who might have posed for one of those pictures of young labor Zionists that I remember from my childhood, those new pioneers who were going to transform Palestine from a barren desert into a fertile paradise for Jews. The portrait was not one that would have appealed to Phil. The son of a Communist Jewish carpenter from the Bronx, he was a left-wing talmudist who would have been far more at home in the college during the depression than during the years of Kennedy's presidency. For Phil sprang full grown from the thirties, and even at City, which was still as close to his instinctive proletarianism (he was the only student I have ever heard who called working-class people proletarians) as any school could possibly have been, he remained an anachronism.

He was the leader of the Marxist Discussion Club. Most students in the club, and there were very few in 1961, were the children of old radicals. A few were engaged in trying to make Marxism more meaningful to their contemporaries, but Phil, who was a tireless worker, was satisfied with things as they were. In the short-story writing course in which I first met him, he emulated the proletarian literature of the thirties. His stories were filled with strikes that were terribly reminiscent of the great C.I.O. strikes of 1937–38; he had cut his eyeeeth on such stories. His point of view was firm; the world of his fiction, like the world in which he presided over meetings of the Marxist Discussion Club, was divided into the "bosses" and the "workers."

He refused to Americanize himself completely, and I rather admired him for this. He spoke excellent Yiddish, usually to me and to the few students who understood him, and in this language he urged invisible groups of workers to "throw off the oppressive chains of the bosses and join together in an expression of worker solidarity." His perorations were magnificent, especially in Yiddish. He liked me, perhaps because I listened to him and argued with him. I could not convince him that his stories lacked realism. If the American worker was no longer the muscular *New Masses* creation of the thirties, that was not Phil's problem. "The day will come when the workers will realize the truth. In the meantime, my stories help create the mold." The worst thing he could call someone was a Trotskyite; to be labeled a bourgeois socialist, which he once called me, was almost as bad. Those old wars had as much meaning for him as they had had for my former chairman at L.I.U.

Because the school had not yet been politicized again in the early sixties, students like Phil stand out more strikingly than they would today. Each student I remember from those years was different. Some possessed passion and energy and commitment, but few were as convinced as Phil of how to apply that passion and energy and commitment. Although the few politicized students were dedicated, their world was split down the center. I remember Lisa, who graduated in 1964, as a girl brimming over with self-confidence, vivacious, in love with Keats and Shelley, even more in love with the idea of serving humanity. She, too, came from a radical family, but both the radicalism and the family were disintegrating. During my first year abroad, I saw an article in the *Times* about how she had been sent packing from a mining town in Kentucky for trying to organize the miners. It was hard to envision her addressing working people. She was always quoting the Romantic poets when she spoke. After that, I heard different stories about her from students and colleagues who had known Lisa. Strangely enough, as the world became more politicized, Lisa turned inside herself. She drifted from group to group and from coast to coast. Now she was living with a journalist in the Village, now with a photographer in Haight-Ashbury. She joined a group who were going to set up a commune in Oregon. Then her money was stolen, she became pregnant, and there was no one to help her get her bearings. Marx soon faded into mysticism. She began to talk about spirits, afterlives, poltergeists. She spent some time in a jail in San Francisco, jilted, broke, and strung out. The deadness at the center, the commitment drying up, the death of Shelley and the rise of Timothy Leary. Lisa was one of the first students who left me wondering why, asking whether the failure lay in her education or in the world she had been told to accept or in her.

Unlike Lisa, Tim was neither argumentative nor political. He was tall and thin, with a face on which that proverbial map of Ireland had been stamped. Whenever he spoke in class, which was not often, his face took on the furtive look I had learned to associate with students in trouble. He could never quite accept the idea that he had a right to his opinions. He would advance whatever he had to say hesitantly, as if he were afraid of being chopped down in the middle of a sentence. And yet he was one of the most brilliant students I have ever taught. His papers were consistently insightful. He was able to bring an intense critical focus to literature, but it evaporated when he had to deal with social relationships. In this he was more representative of the brighter City students than were either Phil or Lisa. People and technology confused him; he was plagued by conscience. For Tim, Camus was not a writer one quoted but a writer one approached with dread and awe. Never have I known a student more willing to let the writer speak for himself, who did not create a critical stance to establish some distance between his world and the writer's. For that would have been a violation of his own selfhood. He wanted to be a teacher but he did not want to go on to graduate school. I suspect he thought it would somehow cheapen his response to writing. Scholarship struck him as trivial and leveling, and while he enjoyed City, he felt that graduate school might trap him. Graduate school demanded a price that Tim was not willing to pay.

It seems to me now that Tim was a victim of the very obscurity endemic to technological man. In this respect, City was kinder to him than the outside world would prove to be. It permitted him to discover that not only did he have a right to his opinions but that opinions were his for the voicing; he did not have to cling to his obscurity, he was capable of making his presence felt. This was more than he had learned either at Cardinal Hayes High

School or in the army, where he had spent three years prior to his arrival at City. If City failed to offer him alternatives to what distressed him in the culture at large, it cannot be faulted for this. He was doomed to failure from the beginning, for he had spent too much energy fighting off his past.

Most of the students I taught during those early years at City were not necessarily tempted to go on to graduate school and further the reputation of their college as one of the nation's better undergraduate institutions. Most simply wanted to reach the point at which they could take care of themselves. Many departed City as they entered it, distrustful of idealism and determined to create a practical compromise with existence. In class they were uncomfortable with Blake's mysticism or Shelley's idealism. Like most pragmatic souls, however, they could appreciate faith in others even if they did not possess it. They managed to create lives for themselves, to seek a limited independence in a world that presented limited rewards.

Most of my students were Jewish, although they were not very aware of their Jewishness. Each class was liberally sprinkled with Italians; there were a few Irish names, a typical New York assortment of ethnic and nationality groups. City always had a large Chinese population, many of whom studied engineering on the north campus. When I remember my early classes at City, I am struck by the absence of black faces among the students. I cannot remember more than one black face in any day session class I taught before 1967, although blacks probably constituted between 10 and 25 percent of the evening session courses I taught. The few black students in the day session seemed to be torn between two worlds and to feel apparently that they could not make lasting connections with either of them. They were veritable caricatures of what white college students were still expected to be in the early sixties, interested in house plans and fraternities and in little else. It was this, more than their color, that made them conspicuous at City.

Their problem was not unusual. Whether the melting pot was merely one more convenient American myth or had some actual historical basis, the fact was that few of my students during the early sixties wanted to be anything other than American. The country they envisaged was destined to become one large happy family, and the strains of "We Shall Overcome" merely confirmed the vision of the nation's destiny. It was just necessary to compromise; one might joke about the world of the WASP, but it was still the world to which all, or almost all, subscribed.

I remember a Puerto Rican student of mine who was typical of many City undergraduates in this respect. He was an excellent student but so totally removed from the street world of the *barrio* that he could not even be accused of having rejected his past; he had simply distorted it by insisting on what he called his "hispanic temperament" and then working very hard to rid himself of all traces of the streets. In 1964 this seemed a logical choice for him, perhaps the only choice. Yet even then he strained under a duality that must have cost him a great deal. He was fixated on the need to prove himself, and he was the hardest-working student I have ever known. Yet he could never escape the need, either as an undergraduate or as a graduate student, to prove that he had a "right" to study English literature. There must have been moments when he felt himself in no-man's-land.

Of all my students, Vito comes most vividly to mind when I think back to those days. He was Italian, and when I first met him as a freshman in 1962, he was the least political creature I had ever known. He simply refused to acknowledge that politics was a form of consciousness. He was interested only in literature, and he struggled to establish a firm relationship with the literary world. He is now completing a Ph.D. in comparative literature on the West Coast. The last time I heard from him was when he sent me a copy of his manifesto for a "new university." A shrill indictment of the modern university, the pamphlet insisted that the university belonged to the people (a proposition with which I certainly could not disagree). The ideals expressed were buried in a self-consciously liberated rhetoric, speaking of a world so totally politicized as to be a fantasy. Here was an indication of how far Vito had come.

I suspect that Vito might have been an anachronism at most other colleges; at City he was not unusual. He possessed a sharp analytical mind, wrote well, and could talk tirelessly about books. He was quiet, but he was also firm. He lacked tolerance, especially for his father, a postal clerk, and his older brother, a Baruch School accounting major. He was sullenly contemptuous of anything that did not pertain to books or culture. He wanted to view life in "perspective," always intent on being a judicious critic. "I'm interested in Dante's Italy, not in Arthur Avenue," he once said to me. And so he pursued his study of languages—Greek, Latin, Italian, French—as well as his study of English literature. In general, he avoided thinking about this country, as he avoided its literature and history. America was the place you escaped from. Not to. From. Never mind what the old man said. All Sicilians were crazy anyway. "With Italians, I trust only northerners. Florentines."

"Cultured people?" I countered.

"Do you want me to blush? It's true."

"I don't want you to do anything."

"I don't believe that. You want me to say yes. Then I become just one more snob escaping from the tenement."

"You don't live in a tenement, Vito."

"What do you know about me, professor? What do you know about any of us?"

He did not like debate. Words were better on paper. He asked questions in class, but he asked them circumspectly, not with that characteristic City College thrust from under intended to put the teacher in his place. He read a great deal, and he once confessed to me he wanted to work his way, sentence by sentence, through *all* of Proust and Joyce and Dostoevsky and Mann. He took my class in short-story writing and wrote two half-formed stories that were emphatically committed in their imagery. The very antithesis of Vito himself. Prose like a runner awkwardly hurdling through the air to throw himself into the fire. Power and hints of grace—enough there to develop. He asked permission to do a creative-writing thesis for his English honors requirement, but his request was denied. "Honors is meant to be a serious scholarly enterprise," the letter read. "While we have, on occasion, permitted a student to substitute a piece of creative writing for the usual scholarly or critical thesis, the Honors Committee does not feel that such action is merited in your case."

After that, he brought his rejection into the classroom. He had become the familiar City student, sitting in class knotted to the edge of his seat, waiting to score his verbal points. Rejection had not blunted the edge of ambition, even if he dropped honors. He would pursue his vision within himself; the rest of the world could be damned.

He had wanted to be the first with the flag, but the island was already claimed. Well, then, he would discover his own island. While I was abroad, he wrote to tell me that he had been in "a bit of trouble" at school. He had been caught taking books from the bookstore. He wanted me to know that he rejected the idea of guilt, rejected it absolutely. He had simply taken "property" from "the system," and those words alone should have told me enough. Before I left, Vito could never have uttered words like that. I suppose he was simply changing with the politics of the day. I received his letter a few weeks after the Berkeley free-speech revolt. He had no regrets about stealing, he wrote, other than having been caught. This country had been built on legalized thievery.

Vito made me understand how student strategies had shifted. There are ways of handling manhood, ways of gratifying individual needs. There are ways of handling reality, too. Vito had always needed heroes and victims. If he was soon to glorify blacks and third world exponents in order to maintain his distance from America, that was simply additional evidence that he had been turned into the country's creature. He had gone, during the time I knew him, from an apolitical student to a politicized student, each of whom read Dante with one eye looking to eternity.

The conversations that I overheard in the student cafeteria in the early sixties were usually more interesting than those in the faculty dining room. The faculty I joined was a peculiar mixture; many of my colleagues seemed preoccupied with a search for style, while others were sincerely coping with the problems of being teachers at City College and with how they could best function in their roles.

Some of the older teachers who had themselves graduated from City in the twenties and early thirties were engaged in the struggle to get beyond their own origins. At one of the earliest department meetings I attended, an issue was raised about the courses to be offered. A slight, stooped figure stood up, a full professor who had a mediocre reputation among the students. In the department he assiduously cultivated the gadfly role, brushing away the dust of the city each summer for bachelor quarters in Paris where he pursued his collection of post-Impressionist paintings. "How do they do it at the better colleges?" he querulously asked. "How do they do it at Harvard?"

He himself had been a student at City in the twenties. It was, no doubt, a particularly cruel fate that had sent him back here to teach, although he was probably more comfortable here than he would have been elsewhere. Somehow the teaching of English had become for him purely a question of style. The academic world was his passport into respectability. How much spontaneity had been deadened in the name of that respectability I could not tell. City had been flooded with spiritual wanderers searching for the higher culture. Style alone could create the proper presence. "How do they do it at the better colleges?" With mirrors, no doubt. He had plunged into the baptismal font and emerged anew.

My own relationship to the faculty was strange. The very physical "feel" of the place testified to its being a bastion of academic respectability, although a crumbling bastion. The dirt-strewn corridors of Mott Hall, the broken plumbing and shoddy surroundings, inevitable but not unattractive. I suspect that in thinking about it today, I have somehow cheapened its reality. The proper atmosphere, no matter how tawdry, creates a home. The need for style is not wholly unattractive. It assumes certain obligations. Its demand for decency and fair play, even its indifference to politics—these have some value in an age that often obliterates reality by ignoring all proprieties. And yet, I could not understand how some of my colleagues could remain oblivious to the very contradictions they embodied. They had lived through the first half of the twentieth century, but they had somehow never permitted it to touch them.

As a young teacher inevitably does, I wanted the acceptance of my older colleagues. And their approval meant more to me than I was willing to admit to myself. It was flattering to discover that City students crowded my classes. What really counted, though, was recognition from my older colleagues, those who had spent a long time in the college community. It was not the search for tenure that sent me seeking their approval. It was simply that any young teacher is bound to measure himself against the possibilities of teaching that he first envisioned as an undergraduate. Despite the observable fact that the majority of his older colleagues are more out of touch with what is happening in the classroom than the young teacher himself, he turns to them for advice and approval. And this was what I did. It was easy enough for me to tell whether a class had gone well or poorly. Students rarely tried to mask their reactions, especially at City. Somehow, though, I was happier when one of the senior faculty observing me for the appointments committee told me after class how pleased he had been with my performance, although were he teaching *In Memoriam,* he might have stressed a somewhat different interpretation from my own. I suppose it was very much like an actor reading his reviews. He knows whether he has given the kind of performance he is capable of giving, but he wishes to have his judgment confirmed by the critics. I knew that I could depend only upon myself and my students to examine what I had done and that all other opinions were essentially of little value. Still I wanted to be told that what I had done had passed muster, made sense to those more "experienced" than I.

By the time I arrived at City, I was a more experienced teacher and was therefore more relaxed in the classroom. And with certain reservations, I felt comfortable with the traditional curriculum. I have never felt particularly comfortable with today's revised curriculum, which offers virtually unlimited "relevance" for faculty and student consumption. To a student body not yet politicized, the old curriculum stood for a social structure in which they still had faith. City College had never been cloistered, yet it was probably closer, in an academic sense, to the mainstream of American life during the early sixties than at any other time in its history. A year of freshman English, which attempted to teach the student to write and to read with critical acumen, was followed by a year of sophomore literature, essentially the same survey of English literature that I had taken at Hunter, except that we began with Chaucer rather than *Beowulf* and concluded with Yeats and Eliot rather than Hardy. To all intents and purposes, I was imposing the same literary structure on my students as had been imposed on me.

I usually taught the second half of the survey, English 4. Possibly because of American pragmatism, I believe that English 4 worked. It certainly worked better than the amorphous courses that have since been substituted for it, in which students choose between genre courses and such plums as "Varieties of Heroism." With all its limitations, the survey offered the student a way into the historical interpretation of literature, and my classes seemed genuinely interested in that. Even students who were to indict Western culture in the years to come, insisting that they did not want the fate of their teachers, enjoyed the idea of the historical continuum that literature provided. I tried to explore both the aesthetic range of English literature and the way in which it had been forced to respond to the problems of our times. In however cursory a fashion, students could witness the evolution of forces that continue to plague and enrich their own lives. Granted that the content to be absorbed was exclusively English literature and that students might want something more immediate, it still provided them with a broad common past to explore. The survey course was far less paternalistic than what was to be substituted for it. I expected my students to define their own meeting ground with the past. The course enabled them to see that there was something beyond their own immediate environments, whereas so many of the courses that were later substituted simply reinforced the idea that their environment was total.

The relevant is not always real. When we reached the point at which we offered courses such as "The Writer and the City," then we had the right to expect that our students would have an idea of what we meant by urban culture. Was this not different from merely having been born in a city or having read a few novels about London or New York or Paris? No matter how one attempted to disguise it, such relevance was intellectualism at its worst. We substituted the new structure of gimmickry and relevance for the historical structure of the survey course. "Compare Dickens' London to Farrell's Chicago." Why not? Wasn't it a mere question of geography? Indeed, why restrict ourselves to Chicago and London? Why not Bangkok and Cairo? If we were really going to bury Western culture, why not do it openly and quickly?

I seem to be endorsing what has come to be called cultural imperialism. And I suppose, too, that because of the guilt that seems to be every American's intellectual heritage today, my objections may easily be misunderstood. Yet had not I, along with so many of my colleagues, accidentally passed into the historical interpretation of literature? Unlike critics forged in the fires of Marxism or the rigorous demands of any other historical ontology, we had no way to synthesize the student's struggle with himself with the collective struggle for cultural continuity. The future had once been claimed by Western man, but students were now questioning all values of the past. In the name of the modern, one could claim anything, embrace any manifestation of cultural disintegration. If we thrust writers against their time in the new relevance that we imposed on our students, we now sought to strip that time of any historical legitimacy. In the process, the legitimacy of imagination was also disposable. English professors once again seemed preoccupied with their own individual style: a useful device to sell rather shoddy wares. Now the men were younger, my own contemporaries. A weary decadence, a sophistication of the moment outside of history, could easily enough be discerned in many of us.

As well as the survey course, freshman composition probably deserves a better defense than I can offer. It provided every student with a year's practice in writing.

142

And no one would argue that the majority of our students did not need practice in putting words together on paper. The teacher's difficulty here lay in discovering some mutual interest that would give the individual student and the class a sense of common purpose. We expected our students to "learn" every kind of writing, from narration to letter writing. And our students themselves were so varied that it was difficult to find problems that were shared by all. Some claimed never to have written a paper in high school, while for others writing was a craft they had been practicing for years. Inevitably, freshman English emerged as a patchwork quilt. It left me puzzled in other respects as well; I really could not understand the assumption of English departments everywhere that a man who earns a graduate degree in English literature automatically knows how to teach young men and women the art of writing. While the value of scholarship, taught to us as an ideal in the graduate school, was real, it was not something that should have been justified pragmatically. And teaching freshman English is undoubtedly the most practical task an English teacher can be asked to deal with. There is nothing in his own training that he can apply to the problems that confront him in the classroom. For here he discovers a land with neither topography nor consistency.

At City, freshman English was a more exciting course than it had been at either N.Y.U. or L.I.U., probably because the students were naturally combative. "Say in class that an adjective modifies a noun, and three students will give you a fight" was an old City College dictum. There was a certain truth to it. Freshman English achieved its greatest triumphs when students tried to fight what it was intended to do, when they resisted the proprieties of language as we teachers advanced them and unconsciously defended a language of innuendo and inflection that was often richer than the accepted forms. When it came to the problems of language, there was an aggressive independence in our students that I grew to cherish; in others, there was a dull willingness to be satisfied with the word as it was written and spoken by their teachers. The majority of my students wrote as if they enjoyed the opportunity to express what they thought.

In general, students complained about freshman English at City as they complained about it elsewhere. Yet they seemed to think it was valuable. It is perhaps unfortunate that they were being asked to get beyond themselves in their writing at a time when they were most eager to delve deeper into themselves personally. The course centered around presenting different methods and styles of writing to the class, but I suspect that my students gained more from personal conferences, where they could go over their papers in detail, than from the classes themselves. Like the survey course, freshmen composition had changed very little since I had taken it as an undergraduate ten years earlier. At a time when change in the academic world is identified with success, this fact sounds suspicious. To remain "static" in the early sixties was among the worst of sins.

I am not quite certain how one measures achievement in teaching freshman how to write. All that I could give my students was certain elementary rules of clarity in writing, which they accepted as they might have accepted instruction in chess, with a certain dry and distant curiosity. They occasionally surprised me, though, in their surrender to the discipline. "I like the comma," said a student to me as we left class one morning. "Sometimes I think I should have lived in the nineteenth century, when the punctuation was closed. You read a novel by Dickens, it's like a map. When you travel certain roads, you look for certain landmarks." I, unfortunately, lacked his passion for the comma or for the rules of order provided by grammar. I did not, I soon realized, really understand what anyone was supposed to be doing in freshman English. And yet I believe that it worked better than I am willing to admit. It did not create the articulateness that we sought in our students, nor did many of them emerge from the course with a sophisticated writing style. It did, however, provide them with a recognition of form, balance, and the knowledge that language must possess its own logic. Its charms were undoubtedly cursory. Nonetheless, a student might learn from it the value of saying what he meant.

English 12 was an introductory course in short-story writing. It was popular with students partly because a large number of would-be writers were attracted to City and partly because the beginning writer was always encouraged to experiment here. In September, 1962, a section of the course was included in my program when one of the regular members of the writing faculty withdrew from the college for the term.

I taught at least one section of English 12 for the next five years, and I knew as little about teaching creative writing at the end of that time as I did at the beginning. My problem was to criticize tactfully and without condescension. Obviously, the same problem confronted teachers speaking about Victorian poetry or thermodynamics. In other courses, however, the material to be dealt with involved the immigration of ideas from the page to the student; the process was clear enough. It did not involve the very fragile ego that the student must nurture and the teacher must protect. In writing, the student's problems, his "sickness," might very well be the substance of his talent and the foundation of his art. He had to be encouraged to repeat the trials and mistakes of writers in the past in his own experience as a writer. He had to learn through his own mistakes without ever taking them personally. He had to deny himself the luxury of an individual ego while, at the same time, he sought a path for his ego to traverse.

I tried to emphasize that there were no guarantees here. Method and style could only be justified by the writer. Writing was a pragmatic act, yet it was an act in which the student ultimately had to declare his own standards of measurement. Whatever information he needed about writing he had to supply himself. Work would be read aloud in class, the writer unidentified, and we would examine what we heard. The good with the bad, turning again and again to the question of whether it worked, of how the language created the effect the writer desired.

I could not explain writing to my students as I might, for example, have explained a literary movement or an intellectual development. Once I accepted the idea that teaching writing was teaching a craft like potting or sculpting, however, I became much happier with what I was able to achieve in the class. I learned to depend upon the "feel" of the thing as a process, yet not to love the product too closely. Blemishes had to be looked at as real blemishes. Above all, I had to be careful not to tell students what they wanted to hear, even those who wanted to hear that they lacked talent, which would relieve them of the burdensome prospect of becoming writers.

If teaching was a craft, then there were certain rules to master. There were also certain indefinite moods that had to be acknowledged. In a sense, the mood of a class was something I could not control; so often the mood was controlled by events, by what was happening "out there." Methodology might be tangible, but I had to realize City College created its own atmosphere, and it had to be considered in dealing with a class. The relationship between teacher, student, and material was inevitably affected by the prison-like Manhattanville Housing Project that we stared at outside the window.

I have never understood exactly why one class got off to a good start, and another, even one composed of many of the same students, was a tooth-grinding battle from its inception. The first advanced literature course I taught was "Emerson and His Contemporaries," and I remember it now as the kind of class teachers speak about being privileged to teach. From the first, I was surprised at the receptivity of the students, at the fact that they were happy to be reading Emerson, happy to discover that the product belied the package. At that time, I probably would have been even happier if I had been asked to teach a course in, say, "American Fiction after World War II." Yet I now believe that there was little that a teacher could offer students in such a course. In nineteenth-century America, the idea of civilization and its discontents was a natural one. Even when I challenged it, I had to react to it, and it offered my students a substance that was lacking in the contemporary. The class might question Emerson's optimism, but this was secondary to the fact that Emerson provided them with a tangible philosophy. When we turned to Melville, to Poe, to Hawthorne, the evil inherent in the American's universe did not descend on us from out of the blue. Emerson had already prepared us for it.

Students at City had certain useful abilities and particular needs that added to the classroom situation. If we were reading Steinbeck's *Grapes of Wrath* and a student brought his guitar to class to play Woody Guthrie's Tom Joad ballad, then this experience might be used to transmit a feeling of the thirties. At City, as at so many other schools, the recent past was most distant from the students. And it was important not to bury the Joads beneath the sentiment of "folksy" protest but to use whatever was available to make the depression come alive in all its reality.

In some respects, that class, the last class I taught at City before my departure for Europe in the summer of 1964, represents for me what teaching was like prior to the rebirth of politics at the school in the mid-sixties. At the risk of generalizing, I would say that the class was intellectually and even socially freer than any I have since taught at City. It was not political, but it had been liberated from the anti-Communist phobia that had infected American life since the late forties. Vietnam had not caught up with us yet. The students seemed to me still essentially part of America, especially when I compare them to those who followed. America was still the ideal for the great majority of them, and it was easy enough to understand why they tried to ignore the Bay of Pigs and the assassination of John F. Kennedy. The possibility of changing things, of restructuring the nation's political life, was real to them; even the one black student in the class insisted on that possibility. During the next few summers, more than a few would be bloodied and disillusioned in Mississippi, in California, in

Kentucky. They would tour America as students in the fifties had toured Europe, though with a different purpose. We had gone for a smattering of culture and out of curiosity about what those ruined monuments actually meant to us; they, on the other hand, were searching their own land for vindication. And when they did not find it, they would return to New York, outraged, furious at the country they had read about in the saga of the Joads because it no longer possessed that primeval vision. Perhaps because they were not really interested in politics in college, they turned on their own innocence with a vengeance in the years that followed. It was undoubtedly to our mutual advantage that neither I nor the students knew what the future had in store for this class. The future at that time seemed as open to them as it did to me. None of us were yet political creatures. We would learn fast.

I received tenure in the department after the usual three-year probationary period, in the spring of 1964. Paradoxically, I learned about school politics at the very time that the larger politics of the nation meant nothing to me. For, once I received tenure, I became eligible to vote in the next election of a new department chairman.

The need for justification was apparently as real in the academic world as it was on Madison Avenue or on Wall Street. Here, too, the key to that need was power. Since the end of the Second World War, academicians had become attuned to the realities and the enjoyment of power. This is the only way I can explain the jockeying back and forth, the wooing of votes, the rhetoric about what kind of department each candidate wanted. Ironically, events were to prove that outside pressures, not the candidates themselves, would shape the future of the department. A candidate might talk of emulating Harvard and Yale, but not even Harvard and Yale would be able to stand on their reputations in a few years. The question of whether a department of scholars or teachers was more desirable became purely academic in the light of the pressures we soon would face. Neither candidate seemed able or willing to view City College in relation to Harlem and New York or even America. They should not be singled out for this failure, however, since no one in the department regarded the college as anything other than a self-contained entity at that time. In fact, few people in the academic world in the spring of 1964 had any idea that American universities and colleges would be called to account in the very near future.

A few days before I left for Europe, I drove up to City to clean out my desk. It was then that I had an inkling of things to come. Harlem had exploded the day before in a riot that signaled the end of the days of "We Shall Overcome." It was mid-afternoon, but the streets were still suppurating from what had happened the night before. The streets were packed with young men and old men and middle-aged men. I pulled over to the curb and got out of my car about a block west of the college, across the street from the housing project. I do not know what I expected, perhaps an accusation that I could parry. There were no revelations to be had here. Feeling foolish and disappointed, I got back into the car. I drove to the college and went through the gate, past the smiling guard. "Man, the shit hit the fan for you guys last night," he said to three policemen who were milling about the entrance. "And you better be ready for it to hit again. It's going to hit again and again and again."

And as I stood on the deck of the *Queen Mary* a few days later, about to embark for a year's appointment at Leiden University in the Netherlands, that guard's face was the memory of the college I carried with me. The myth and the reality were preparing to face each other. And though I was not prepared to argue with that gallery of the children of immigrants who would defend their alma mater, I shivered with the thought that I might be asked to choose sides in the future. For I did not know which side I could claim as my own.

Chapter Six

The ten-month Fulbright year abroad at Leiden University was filled with Dutch pomp and circumstance. For the Dutch, I must have seemed a plebian storming the fortress of European culture, and visions of young American academic mercenaries laying siege to this old Europe probably spun through their heads. How tired they were of defending a culture they no longer believed in. Unspoken questions: what do you know of our culture, young man? And what did I know? Did I really understand their heritage? The sickness of futurism suddenly takes on new life as a car stops before an old crumbling gate house on a lonely road and a vapid-eyed motorcyclist spins off a drawbridge with his America, his Russia, his China, everything but his Europe, under his leather jacket. Here was the new Europe, my long-lost paradise!

It was all very impressive. The Academiegebouw, where I delivered my twice-weekly lectures, had been filled with students more than thirty years before Henry Hudson and his sailors on the *Halve Maen* approached the Palisades. The stones in the courtyard, the tower thrusting itself against the Rapenburg, the stark illuminating presence of the Pieterskerk in the square across the canal, the statue of Boerhaave that I drove past on the way to my office, even the damp musty smell of my office forced me to question. Was I simply one more American apostle come to be reconverted? Was I another returning stranger begging to confront the natives and to be informed of his legitimacy? Even trips to Dachau would not change that quest. A pistol in the mind exploding memories of unknown cousins and aunts and uncles and grandmother and grandfather, symbols of this Europe, too. The soft legitimacy of Goethe, who had puffed up my undergraduate vision of the universal man, of Mann's stentorian overtures to my soul. ("Students here do not read Mann any longer," said my Dutch poet friend to me as we sat in the Indonesian restaurant in Leiden. "But perhaps that is not so bad, is it? We don't like things German.") Home of the eternal student, the intellectual Alpine wanderer moving through realms of books, worlds of mind and desolation and surfeit. Was this what I had offered my students at City? This the common heritage that I asked them to call their own?

Was this even the European past about which I had dreamed? This genteel, introverted university that was as beckoning as a Forty-second Street movie marquee. The professorial discourses, the argumentative snobbery, the belief that America had seized it all, and the desire to repay America by emulating her until she cried "Enough!" No doubt it was merely another fantasy fabricated by the academic world. Yet I could not help but feel they were taking their revenge upon Columbus for his mistake, for his horseshoe swindle of these old universities.

The professors themselves readily admitted that they did not work very hard. There was no need to; working hard was not among their obligations. All they were supposed to do was run the institute. Perhaps I should have looked closer. Perhaps here was the future model for the American urban university. The institute with which I was officially affiliated had been designed to explore Dutch-English cultural relations. It was staffed by men whose test of literacy seemed to be the impeccability of an English accent. The difficulty lay, however, not in the pomposity or even in what might legitimately be called the narrow circumference of the scholarship itself—and not merely by me but by the European intellectuals and scholars Auerbach and Curtius and Lukačs, whom I had been taught to revere—but rather in the aridity of the high culture that was displayed here like a collection of rare peacock feathers.

Europe's revenge manifested itself in the students, too. They seemed remarkably tame, particularly after my students at City. Here they would not challenge a teacher even if he resorted, in an attempt to inspire some reaction, to a hortatory sermon on the needs of the young. "If one resists the traditional idea of culture, then it very well may turn out that art and the culture are the healthier for it."

"We have been trained to listen. We cannot resist, sir."

And was it enough to blame it on the gymnasia, on that vast array of "trained" minds lined up against these post-war European students like machine guns? Or was it better to blame it on the European culture, on the way in which even Nietzschean idol-smashing had become ritualized, on the dreadful formalism that strangled the students' possibilities? In any case, it was not particularly exciting teaching after City College, and while the year itself proved to be a rich one for me, teaching seemed a different profession, an occupation enjoyed by others. Europe, however, had preened herself for me that year, had presented herself to my view with both scars and monuments intact. Europe was willing to let me enter through the heavy portals so long as I could afford the price of admission. The guilt I felt in Holland from working so little and traveling so much was alleviated by the fact that the majority of my Dutch colleagues worked even less and traveled more.

There are causes waiting even for wandering professors. When I left for Europe, Vietnam had been a name on a map; when I returned, it was thrust before me as the knife that would sever American academic life in two. During my year in the Netherlands, I remember speaking about the war only twice, each time with a Dutch intellectual who voiced his dispassionate approval of American actions. I was for getting out, but our fighting there seemed to me a mere mistake in policy that could easily be rectified. I should have known better. The Bay of Pigs should have taught me that. At that point, however, it did not seem to have very much to do with my professional life or interests.

College teachers today are wont to believe that the world of the university makes up the totality of American life and that if the schools' problems can be solved, then the problems facing the nation at large can somehow be solved. I knew that this was not true, and yet within a year so absorbed was I in what was happening at City that I could not help but feel that it was true. In the years to come, any lingering illusions that the colleges were at the peripheries of national life were shattered for everyone. Berkeley had been the shot fired round the academic world, and it brought home a reality that we had chosen to ignore for more than two decades. While I was abroad, my sympathics were with the Berkeley students. Of course, I was far away. And I happily accepted that distance. There had been moments in which what I read about the students' protests was made real to me, such as an hour spent with a professor of history from Berkeley with whom I had been interviewing candidates for Woodrow Wilson fellowships. I remember how his voice filled with emotion when he told me of what had happened, of the letters he had received describing the events on campus that winter. He himself liked Mario Savio. He understood the positions of the students. Still, universities had their own needs and obligations. "I really feel for those kids. Much of what they say is true. But what do they expect of us? What is it that they want us to do?" We sat in the hotel drinking Danish beer until he looked at his watch and took his leave. He had to catch a plane to Washington, where he was to spend a week in what he called "a consultative capacity for the Pentagon."

And yet how would I have changed it, if I could have? It would be dishonest to write that I immediately began thinking about the relationship of government, military, industry, and university in American society. In Europe I was not thinking about very much at all; I had cast heritage aside.

In America, on my return, I discovered that the extreme style was spreading throughout the City campus, a quick reaction to the growing politicalization of American colleges and universities. The antiwar movement had wiped away whatever remnants of political fear and lethargy still existed. It was necessary to take sides. The extreme style was inevitable; it contained so much bottled-up energy, so many years of frustration and silence, that it could only find release in a steady barrage of radicalized rhetoric. In order to keep your just-won radical credentials respectable, you raised the verbal ante. Even to express it this way, though, is to cheapen recent consciousness and experience. For Vietnam was transformed before our eyes into a reality that consistently managed to make the rhetoric inadequate. No matter which way I turned, no matter how I tried to examine the rhetoric coolly and dispassionately, the reality was always one step ahead, each time leaving me amazed and angered and wanting desperately not to believe the cameraman and news reporters.

When I returned to the college, the sense of place was different. Everything was magnified. What had once been minor irritants—the shoddy toilets, the drab student cafeteria, the crowded facilities for study—mushroomed in my mind. I felt irritated with the college, with the students, with the country. It was a debilitating summer, my first experience at teaching only the night session. And the night-school student lived in a world in which the college and its demands were peripheral. I should have welcomed this change, but I didn't. The élan of the day-session students was missing here. Essentially, there were two kinds of night-session students: nonmatriculants attempting to work up the necessary credits so that they could matriculate in the day session, and matriculating older adults, anywhere between twenty and forty years old, who worked during the day and took between six and nine credits per term at night, carrying a grueling schedule, determined to improve themselves both financially and intellectually.

It was uneven teaching, for the classes were even more temperamentally and intellectually disparate than those I had taught during the day. Young men and women who had no idea of why they were in college, sitting side by side with others capable of making extraordinary sacrifices for the opportunity of learning. The nonmatrics generally apathetic, unsure of themselves yet not sufficiently afraid of failure to reach down and push themselves harder; the older people dreaming of getting out of marginal employment areas, sometimes dreaming of the world of learning that lay before them, beckoning them on, making them aggressive and humble at the same time. New immigrants in the City tradition.

Classes at night lacked cohesiveness; they seemed to form themselves, and there was little that the teacher could do to make them into a unit. Dissimilarities of aim and purpose, ambition struggling against reality. Teachers floated through the classrooms like Chagall peasants; students and teachers saw each other as contemporaries. In the day session, one was either this or that, radical or conservative; at night, a student could be both a political radical and a member of a house plan.

The students in the day session seemed different that September, too. Yet they were the same students who had made my Emerson class so memorable. They now had difficulty working. "It's purposeless," said one of my former students who had dropped into the office. "I used to love this place. I used to find it exciting. You know what I do now? I spend all of my time in the snack bar. And we don't even talk about anything there." I didn't know how to be sympathetic. Even in late 1965 the war was affecting all of us more than anyone then realized. The most sensitive students seemed uniformly listless. The future seemed both distant and unpromising. They found work in their undergraduate classes tedious, even those who had come bursting into my office a year earlier to tell me about a poet just discovered or to read me something they had written. The texture of life at the college had already been politicized. For many students, City had evolved into the visible manifestation of all that was wrong with the country.

The mood foretold a return to the college's past. More than most other colleges in the country, City had been forced to live down its 1930s reputation that had earned it the sobriquet "The Little Red School House." If the majority of students were not particularly aware of what this could mean for the college, the faculty was, especially those professors who had been at the college for more than a decade. It had been no more than eight years since teachers had been pulled out of classrooms by the guardians of the college's faith and morals. City had since set out to earn political respectability. Political gestures, even gestures that might be open to political interpretation, made people nervous at City. I remember a friend of mine asking me to help her sell some emblems for a Japanese peace group. At lunch I took the pins out of my pocket and asked some colleagues if they wanted to buy them. They didn't refuse. They simply ignored me and went on talking. Later that afternoon I mentioned the incident to another colleague who had been at the college since the early fifties. "Have you thought of what you were asking those people?" he said. "Each of them has seen teachers taken out of classrooms. They witnessed the kind of red-baiting on this campus that you'd expect to find in the *Daily News*. One of them was a student here during the thirties. Don't judge them. The only thing we want to retain from our radical decade is the names of our respectable alumni. We're a different school now, part of a university. We choose administrators because of their respectability. We cite statistics indicating how we have more graduates going on for their Ph.D.'s than any other school in the country, and our students are known for the number of Wilsons they win each year, not for their politics. Ask these same men to subscribe to a scholarship fund, and you'll see what kind of response you'll get. They're not ungenerous. It's just that they're close enough to what happened on this campus during the fifties to make them exceedingly cautious. They think they have a great deal to risk. And don't you be virtuous at their expense."

Their memories were still raw and threatening. And he was right. I could not judge them, for I had not lived through the same experiences. And if I ever were to live through something similar, I had no way of knowing whether I could hold on to what I believed.

When the school's climate seemed safe enough to venture political opinions in public once again, the faculty did so with a vengeance, however. "Don't ever ask me anything like that again, Leonard," said one of my luncheon companions a few days after I had tried to sell him a pin. "I don't appreciate political solicitation at lunch." Six months later he scolded me for not having sought out his signature for a protest advertisement

against the war in the *Times.* By the end of 1967, I could
have passed around a petition calling for virtually anything and received signatures from many of the faculty.
The years had made commitment a raging fashion in
academia. The faculty felt obligated to follow the lead
of the students. And the students were protesting the
war, the draft, the R.O.T.C. program, and virtually every
affiliation of college and government. The faculty hustled
after them, struggling to keep up.

The protest against the war was genuine enough. It
represented a growing sense of outrage, the belief that
we all, students and faculty alike, had been lied to, duped,
and ridiculed by the government—our government. No
one could claim that we had lost perspective, for the war
was even more duplicitous, even more sickening, even
more immoral than we maintained. Somehow we felt
obligated to use the intelligence and sensitivity of our
students as our own; we seemed to feel that we had to
follow them. Our protest, our outrage, like so much else,
had been created out of the exigencies of the moment.
We were not so much interested in truth, even the sordid
truth about Vietnam, as we were in vindication. And
it was the students whom we chose as vindicators. In our
zeal to be loved, we made history outlandish by turning
it into an all-encompassing metaphor for cruelty. We
used the word *genocide* to describe everything from
Vietnam to questions of whether college administrations
had the right to call police on campus. The students demanded liberation; we demanded it with them, although
we were never quite certain of what it was *we* wanted
to be liberated from.

Students grew more demanding and rhetorical. And
the professors who sympathized with them followed

their lead. I found myself addressing large rallies of students protesting the war. The words gushed forth: Thoreau, the impeccable gesture at the necessary time, waves of applause and flashes of bodies dying in green jungles—ours and theirs, bodies. I grew to like such public performances at the very same time that I despised myself for liking them. It annoyed me that I responded to the idea of becoming a celebrity among the students. Still, I responded. And while my hatred of the war was real enough, at least a small portion of my militancy was due not so much to the desire to change this country—although that was always primary—but to the need to develop a mask for myself. Not a mask to meet my colleagues. A mask to meet my militant students.

I remember addressing a crowd of students in Finley Student Center in the fall of 1965. I remember trying to be analytical at first, to condemn a policy rather than a country, to dissect an idea of nationhood rather than to voice another slogan condemning the United States. As I continued speaking and could feel the support of the packed auditorium of students sitting in front of me, the temptation to thrust myself, or rather an image of myself, forward became almost irresistible. Suddenly I was not speaking to them but at them, and I was excited by the idea that I had them, that I could do with them whatever I wished. The naked temptation of rhetoric. I was filled with a sense of my own power; I was able at this moment to impose my interpretation of the world upon a large gathering. I was using the students. When I left the platform, I felt surfeited with the power of language, my own language. I had been offered the apple by the snake, and I had taken as deep a bite as anyone else. I had been rewarded with applause from an auditorium filled with over four hundred students. I had created my militant mask. And I wore it like a schoolyard hero.

The temptation to politicize everything, even social relationships within the college, grew geometrically in the next few years. The college, along with the political situation in the country, made it possible to externalize all relationships in terms of politics. It was a peculiar academic myopia that I shared with many members of the faculty who, like me, considered themselves men of the Left. In 1966 and 1967 the men of the Right were visible but more often than not silent. The Center served as our enemy. If we conducted ourselves with a great deal of self-righteousness, as we undoubtedly did, the Center conducted itself with an incredible obliviousness to reality. The professors in this camp covered themselves with an academic shield that had long since tarnished; they were pursuing the logic of the times down the long, dusty corridors of truth. Inevitably, they came to justify both the college administration's conduct of affairs at City and the national administration's conduct of the Vietnam War. As the militant students insisted that the faculty join them now rather than in the future, the faculty continued to splinter. The Right remained adamant, frequently in the name of civil liberties. One of the more repellent ironies of the time was that men who had acquiesced in the intellectual repressions of McCarthyism were now lecturing their colleagues like fervent members of the American Civil Liberties Union. "We have to see Vietnam in a larger perspective. I'm not *for* our policy there, mind you. It's just that I'm not quite certain that we have any alternatives." And the Left came to the defense of the students. Even when their demands indicated that they were novices in the academy and knew very little about how it worked, we did not protest. Criticism was rocked to sleep by love.

I suspect that we turned to the students because they restored us to a belief in moral simplicity. They were not altogether right, but they were passionate. They were not judicious, but they were dedicated. They were not compromisers; they were idealists. They were not worldly, but they were fighters. If they could sometimes be accused of creating issues out of thin air, they could not be faulted for shirking responsibilities, as could the college administration, which wanted only not to make waves. We defended the students, angered by the administration. We identified with our students, though we only claimed to be defending their right to see the world as they wished to see it. For us, the sins of the fathers were not to be visited upon the children. Instead, their sins were to be made into our absolution. Their passion would create our identity. And their destiny was to mold our passion, to motivate us with fundamental perceptions that we could no longer share. Even when the student passion sprang from ignorance, it was still possible to go along with that passion. Although we claimed to believe in a Thoreauvian moral stance, too many of us surrendered conscience to those students willing to serve as our moral caretakers.

Even when we managed to remove ourselves from a vision of the militant young as moral exemplars, we were inevitably forced to follow their lead because of the manipulative distortions of the administration. No matter how overstated the case that the students presented, the administration somehow managed to make that case both rational and supportable. A minor varia-

tion on Vietnam. Charges flew, denials were made, and
then the reality of the situation proved to be remarkably
close to what the students had originally said it was. This
does not, of course, excuse those of us who were not as
honest with our militant students as we should have been.
It does explain the persistence of our failure. The "hut
controversy" was an excellent example of how this took
place.

The controversy was typical of City and typical of
the restlessness that had come to characterize the relationship of students, faculty, and college administrations
throughout the country. The controversy was farcical in
itself, but it was representative of things to come. This
was the last time that an issue animated radical and
nonradical students at the college with a similar sense
of purpose; at the same time, the event marked the end of
the loose alliance of radicals and liberals that had sprung
up on campus. Like the Columbia insurrection of April,
1968, the crisis transcended its cause.

In 1966 the administration had announced construction
plans for the college designed to alleviate the pressure
upon the overburdened physical plant. Of course, we
were skeptical when the huts were labeled "temporary
structures," yet we were sympathetic to the president's
plan. After all, the college's well-publicized master plan of
1964 had set February, 1966, as the completion date for
the science and education building for which ground had
not yet been broken in 1967. There was an obvious need
for any new facilities that would alleviate the crush. The
building of the huts promised new classroom and office
space that we desperately needed. If the issue had been
merely the location of those "temporary structures," I
doubt that it would have caused such furor on campus.

However, when the college administration called in the police to arrest nine student protesters on October 5, 1967, the entire college was thrown into turmoil. The students' case, on the face of it, left a great deal to be desired, as even those of us who sympathized with them had to admit. The students had objected to the uprooting of trees and to the destruction of one of the last grassy areas left on the campus. It was growing more and more difficult for a student not to feel physically constricted at City. There were lines even for using the toilets. Frustrated by the college's refusal to acknowledge their need for space, the students sat in the trees—a Chaplinesque gesture of defiance—until the police were called to pull them out and arrest them. The students could not deny that the college desperately needed classroom and office space, and their claim that they had not been consulted about the sites for the huts was ludicrous. The protest was ill-conceived and poorly timed. The truth was largely on the side of the administration this time.

Yet the students had focused on needs that many younger members of the faculty were beginning to recognize. The sense of dissatisfaction that so many of us felt stemmed from our belief that the administrative bureaucracy lacked any idea of what it meant by an *education*. The members of the college's administration seemed to believe that the way to deal with crises or handle problems was to reduce them to the most meaningless possible denominator, substituting pious platitudes for a sense of purpose. It was not so much that the administration had called police on campus but that even the action of calling the police meant nothing to the administration. It was becoming evident that the college existed for its administrators alone; the community of scholars and the community of students might yet be displaced by the school's administrative bureaucracy.

The placement of the structures was actually a symbolic issue, and a rather poor one at that; the real issue was that student activists and their sympathizers, as well as the majority of younger faculty, no longer had any faith in the administration. It is impossible for any institution to function without this faith. It was not so much that they distrusted the president of the college. Rather, it became apparent, as the administration vacillated between pieties and half-hearted demands for order on the campus, that those in charge cared nothing for the activists and merely felt students were better seen and not heard. As other issues emerged, the college's future began to take shape. The S.E.E.K. program, still in its early stages, had generated strong support among black students, who looked upon the program as a way of getting more blacks into City. The president of the all-black Onyx Society charged that the student protest against the site facilities was a "deliberate impediment to education that must be considered racism." However ill-conceived the charge might seem to the student protesters, it appealed to black students at the college and to residents of Harlem alike. "If Whitey really wanted us to go to college, he'd give us that school up there on the hill." The students' objections to the removal of trees made no sense to people desperately seeking to send their children to college. The administration, eager to use whatever ammunition it had, began to play up the theme of how the student activists were interfering with the possibilities for expansion and for accommodating the S.E.E.K. program. This was the first conflict at the college where white and black had been played off against one another. Even then it was evident that this incident might set a pattern for the animosities that would explode during the next few years. Quite abruptly, the problem on campus shifted from the question of facilities to the question of who was and who wasn't a racist.

Suddenly the college was flooded with rumors about its future. The combined S.A.T. and high school average scores of City's applicants were now the lowest of the four municipal colleges. If you wanted a future in college teaching, then it was time to get out, escape to the Graduate Center at Forty-second Street. Throughout 1967–68, the college seemed to be disintegrating, it no longer remembered the function it was supposed to perform. Its function, however, remained exactly the same as it had been outlined by Townsend Harris back in 1847: to educate the people of the city. The people of the city had grown darker, but this did not change the school's function.

The issue of race in academic life was unlike any other issue, for no one wanted to deal with it. It threatened us in a way that no other issue, not even Vietnam, had threatened us, and it evoked in the faculty essentially one of two responses. On one hand, there were those who believed that to be black automatically ensured absolution from the moral crises of the age. In the years to come, I was to hear the term *racist* randomly hurled at too many people who did not deserve it, used as a club to intimidate opposition, and to shatter the subtle edge of hysteria, in a peculiar inversion of "law and order." On the other hand, there were those who remained aloof from the very real problems and aspirations of young blacks, convinced that the presence of black students actually threatened to destroy the college.

168

They insisted that unless blacks were willing to accept traditional academic standards, there was no way of salvaging the college. There was no reconciling the two camps.

Strangely enough, no one appeared interested in the constituency who needed City College and the services it could provide. The vast majority of white students at City were faced with a simple choice: attend one of the free municipal colleges or do not go to college. Neither they nor their parents could conceive of alternatives; it was "free" education or no education at all. Categorizing all of them as members of the middle class, as more of my colleagues were now beginning to do, simply made the concept of class ludicrous. There may have been some students who drove cars to college and frantically competed with one another for parking spaces, but they were heavily outnumbered by students who rode bikes. And 99 percent of the students still traveled to the college by subway. The new middle class: fathers who were cab drivers, supermarket clerks, subway conductors, electricians, minor civil servants, owners of run-down candy stores. And even the fathers, trying to keep one step ahead of escalating inflation and the demands of consumerism, accepted their new status.

Again, the college emulated the nation. America was not yet willing to take from those who could afford it. It was easier to label all whites middle class and leave it at that. White students at the college were suddenly discovering that they were no longer the salt of the earth. Men who sent their own sons to Harvard were demanding that City's white students make room for blacks. "What do they want from my ass anyway?" asked a militant student soon after the hut controversy. "No matter what I do, I'm a godamn honkey. Man, I'm getting tired of showing my credentials."

It was another problem that the college had not yet faced. The college was not the only guilty party. For the nation had not faced it either. Who, after all, could pay the price for 350 years of oppression and injustice? If black and white were going to fight over possession of City, the inevitable was no more than just. Obviously the blacks had to have the college, and the whites, most of whom were Jews anyway, would have to give it up. (The mood coincided, and not by accident, with the rise of a simplistic political anti-Semitism in the American Left.) Suddenly nothing was more appealing than the prospect of playing black. Every few years we simply traded in one victim for another. We could wash down the radical psyche as we washed away the stain of color. No doubt, given the rules of the game, radicals could trade in blacks for Indians or Chicanos in a few years' time. It was a peculiar Left that now spoke at the college, one that was angrier at Jewish cabbies and Irish cops than at the Rockefellers. The "real" rich, at least, had the grandeur of wealth and the sweep of expectancy. And what could be more exciting to the heart of the intellectual?

No one knew what argument to use when blacks insisted on the prerogatives of color. There were few real Marxists among the faculty Left; had we been Marxists, perhaps we might have been able to adopt a consistent intellectual position, in which class rather than race was the determining factor. Ultimately this lack of a position made things difficult for us. How could we defend the prerogatives of color without opening the gates to white ethnics who would claim their territories, too? No member of the faculty felt that he could protect his world convincingly. No matter how sympathetic I might be to the demands of blacks and Puerto Ricans, no matter how aware I might be of the growth of discontent among Jews at the college, the truth was that I no longer knew where I stood. Ideally, I suppose, I wanted a college that would permit me to stand in all corners.

Meanwhile, however confused and uncertain, I continued with what I was doing, although I was a mass of contradictions. It was not just going to be difficult to be both pro-black and pro-white working class; there were indications that it might prove to be impossible. I remained sympathetic to those who were demanding special programs for black students. I might have been irritated by the rhetoric of black power, yet I could see the undeniable substance behind the rhetoric. Black students *were* being discriminated against, if not by City in particular, then by the society of which City was representative. The blacks on campus, both students and faculty, were justifiably dissatisfied. (There were still very few black faculty in 1968, one of the sources of the dissatisfaction among students.) A black student whom I had known since 1965 said to me, "When I came here, I just wanted to be like everybody else. Now I'm getting rid of that being-white business. It's not that I believe any of that crap about my being superior. No matter how many dashikis I wear, you still know more than me. But I'm beginning to discover that Whitey can go to hell and it won't make any difference unless I can live with myself."

In September, 1968, at the behest of a close friend in

the department, I taught a single section of freshman English in the pre-baccalaureate program, known as S.E.E.K. The program had originated at the college in September, 1965, with 109 students from New York City's black and Puerto Rican ghettos. The experiment attempted to take young men and women with a high school diploma whose averages would ordinarily not have been sufficient for admission to the college, offer them financial aid and psychological guidance as non-matriculated students, and then absorb those who were successful into the college's degree-granting program. By the time I taught in the program, it had grown from the original 109 to well over 500 students, not counting those who had already dropped out or passed to the baccalaureate stage. In the municipal university system, there were plans for accepting a total of 3,500 S.E.E.K. students each year, with an ultimate goal of a total S.E.E.K. enrollment of 10,000.

A group of younger teachers, half of them black (at that time, the regular English department had only one full-time black member), had been hired to teach exclusively in the S.E.E.K. program. In a program that would test one's endurance, one's patience, and one's talent as nothing before had done, an evangelical zeal to teach was a necessity. I admired and envied the spirit and dedication I witnessed in most of the S.E.E.K. teachers.

The S.E.E.K. teaching staff was directed by a woman who had joined the department that September. She was one of the few people I had ever met who had actually thought about the problems involved in teaching essentially noncommunicative students how to write, how to grasp the idea that communication itself required logic and assertiveness. She was to spend her time with students

who now had to be made aware of their right to formulate opinions and their obligation to formulate them
thoughtfully and intelligently. Time and again during
our staff meetings, she would force us to concentrate
on the problems of teaching these students. From her
point of view, they were the beginning and end of our
academic responsibility and purpose. Whenever any of
us turned away from these problems to speculate on the
meaning of the program, she would gently but forcibly
bring us back to our students and their seemingly mundane world. No quest for the higher purpose for her.

She had a single thought in mind: to educate. She
had little patience with political rhetoric, but she had
great tolerance and an enormous feeling for the S.E.E.K.
students, the peculiar intensity of feeling that leads a
poet to embrace the idea of reality itself. Although she
wished to guard the program from those intent on preach-
ing diatribes, she realized that it was essential that our
students change their images of themselves and of their
capabilities. Wary of any tendencies toward illusion and
self-deception in herself, she would not tolerate them in
others. For her, mastery of the art of communication was
revolutionary. She was willing to ride with the minds and
imaginations of her students. If they opted for revolution,
they would have to create one. Suspicious of abstractions
in any form, she insisted on paying attention to immediacies, to leave the self alone for quiet nurturing.
She wanted to give her students the power to command
language, to say what they meant. "Which perfume to
use in the morning can be a meaningful choice, too."
Obviously it could. Yet it had been a long time since
anyone at City College had dared to admit so immediate
a truth.

Her sense of what was real kept her sane and made her

an effective teacher and administrator. While some of the teachers in the program discussed who was and who was not a racist, she moved quietly through the naked immediacies of City College. She was able to drive herself with incredible diligence, and she shamed others into making the effort their students required of them. She insisted that a teacher always be himself in a classroom, for she valued the unpredictability of the human. And yet she had limited expectations. A paper with fewer mechanical errors, a more confident tone, greater coherence of thought and language—this was a teacher's reward. The S.E.E.K. students were fortunate to have her; the college was even more fortunate.

My first weeks teaching in the S.E.E.K. program were both enlightening and discouraging. I had never really thought very much about what language did to the poor and the black. Although I looked upon the art of writing as the formal organization of language into coherent sentences and paragraphs, virtually all my S.E.E.K. students looked upon it as additional confirmation of failure and ineptitude. Of course, students in regular freshman English classes who were not particularly good writers felt the same way, but they usually had something to fall back on—an ability to draw, perhaps a flair for biology or for the jargon of the social sciences—and so they were able to disguise their ineptitude with language. This experience was different. Here was a sense of massive intellectual failure that stemmed from caste, emanating from a sense of worthlessness that raked black students over the coals existing in America. Language was gesture, but for these students, gesture was still derived from the streets. Even speaking was more of a threat than a promise, perhaps because of the richness of street language. Yet their problem with words was not so much different as accentuated. It had also been that way among the friends with whom I had grown up; they too had looked on language as a peculiar richness of their own until forced to translate, to turn it into an instrument of conscious communication. These students did not lack opinions, I discovered, but their New York City educations had taught them to guard their opinions, to use language for dissimulation rather than refinement of thought. From the point of view of my students, my job was to teach them how to make their words drip with the sweet fat of bureaucracy (*there* was money in the bank, what *they* paid you for) and tie them together with the formal structures designed to disguise the soul.

There were fourteen students in the class. (Classes were kept to a maximum of fifteen, whereas the regular freshman English classes averaged closer to twenty-four students.) I remember how strange I felt as I introduced myself on that first morning. In six years of teaching full-time at City during the day session, this was the first class that I had had with more than two black faces in it. The class was composed of eight blacks, four Puerto Ricans, a Mexican girl, and a young Jewish mother of two. I spoke about what the course was designed to do, what I expected of them, and listed the texts we would be using. For their first assignment, I asked them to describe Canova's *Perseus Holding the Head of Medusa*, which had been unveiled one week earlier at the Metropolitan. I wanted a simple descriptive paper that would tell me what mechanical problems these students faced.

I succeeded, perhaps beyond my own expectations. Among other things, I discovered that a number of my students didn't know where the museum was, although they had all been New Yorkers for at least ten years. Their problems in writing were so elementary that I began to wonder whether I could really blame the much-abused public schools. Where did I begin? On what would I focus? On the day on which the first papers were due, a Puerto Rican student in the class entered my office with a remarkably ornate story of how he had been unable to get to the museum. He had been one of the two most articulate students in class during that first week. This was the first time I had confronted this particular problem. I had known many students who were afraid to put words down on paper, but here I had a student who was frightened of going to the museum. Not knowing how else to handle it, I told him to bring the paper in the following day or else not bother coming to class. I had no desire to punish; I simply didn't know how else to approach his problem. There were undoubtedly better ways, but I was lucky. In his case, I hit the right key. He brought the paper in the next day, eyed me angrily all through class, and was, by the term's end, one of the best students in class. I would imagine that many of my S.E.E.K. students, and others at the bottom of the economic scale, were so used to speaking about their problems that they tended to hang on to them rather than to seek solutions.

The night I read that first batch of papers probably represents the nadir of my career as a college teacher. I had expected the grammatical errors and the errors in syntax. I had not been prepared for the way in which racial consciousness seemed to obscure everything else. "When I see this statue it is of the white man and he is holding the head of the Negro."

About a week later, a twenty-seven-year-old former

army sergeant followed me to my office after class. He wanted to speak about something that was troubling him. He sat down next to my desk and began telling me about his experiences as a brick layer in the construction industry in New York. "I'm dropping history," he announced in the middle of a sentence.

"Why?"

"I don't know enough." He shook his head, then shrugged. "I feel so goddamn ignorant. You don't know what it feels like to sit there. I'm twenty-seven. I'm twenty-seven and I sit there and I want to cry like a baby." I suggested a few books he might read for some background, and I wound up convincing him not to drop history. I suspect he had convinced himself and had come to me for confirmation. And from that time on, he represented the class for me.

It had happened before. There are classes in which you address yourself to one or two students. Through them, you hope that you can connect with the rest of the class, although you are never quite sure why. From that time on, I was talking to that one student. And while I hoped that the other thirteen were listening, I was not particularly sanguine about their prospects. After that first paper, I jotted down the names of the students I expected to fail. Eight out of fourteen. Not a very encouraging prospect. During the weeks that followed, I discovered that their chief problem was neither grammar nor syntax. Their problem was to permit themselves an opinion, to learn to use the very perceptions that the ghetto had given them. Ghettos, of course, teach one to tread carefully. And no one, certainly no white professor, was going to convince these students in a few weeks that the quality of their own experience and their own information was valuable and useful in dealing with issues that confronted them daily.

Not all the problems were theirs. One of my own was accepting the idea that they really weren't very different from their white peers. I soon found myself fighting the temptation to believe that blacks could revive America's long-dormant revolutionary virtues. I wanted to set about the task of remaking America, and I suppose that, to be honest, this was one of the principal reasons I was teaching in the S.E.E.K. program. These students, though, wanted in to this system. "I want what Whitey's got," said the former brick layer. Significantly enough, white students were just beginning to express their reservations about American acquisitiveness. My S.E.E.K. students, however, smelled success in the air. Curiosity was a luxury; the civil service beckoned. The girls in the class all wanted to become teachers, to attain success as the working and lower-middle classes have traditionally measured success. They reminded me of the girls I had known at Hunter. "Teaching is a good job for a girl until she gets married." The presence of Dow Chemical recruiters on campus had become an issue for the rest of the college as the war in Vietnam heightened. My S.E.E.K. students remained apathetic to the issue, despite the fact that Vietnam had been a reality to their brothers and sometimes to them. They remained indifferent or apathetic to issues unless they were issues of race. Even there, they met me with a skeptical eye. They tolerated this kind of probing only in class. Success was a more traditional American motivation than protest. Stereotypes were being turned on their heads. And they were not going to feed my illusion of transforming American life in an updated W.P.A. spirit of black America, all muscle, bone, and fire.

"What should a black student do in a white school?" asked the sincerely puzzled student at the meeting.

"Burn it down!" cried the editor of the militant monthly.

"Shit," muttered the student sitting next to him.

Nor could I decide which voice spoke most honestly for black America. That question, of course, had nothing to do with me. Neither I nor my white students were going to be "saved" by playing castle virgin waiting for the good black knight. My job was simply to teach these students how to write a paper. By the first week in November, I was still discouraged. Grammar and syntax had improved considerably, but, with two or three exceptions, I was still getting the kind of papers that were not even worthy of a high school class. "Of all the different ideas, I think that the very best, aside from Father's Day, is Mother's Day." What could I do with that?

In mid-November the papers began to change in tone and in the interests they reflected. Perhaps it had simply been a question of time, of the students permitting themselves to speak about what they were really interested in. Perhaps it had been a question of trust, and they had spent all this time sizing me up. Suddenly they were interested in the world around them, were brimming over with opinions about the future that loomed over them, about campus unrest, about threats and possibilities. A young girl came to ask me whether she could write a biographical study of Malcolm X. She had once worried about what people—and by that she meant white people—would think about blacks after listening to Malcolm. But she had just finished reading his *Autobiography* and . . .

That term I learned that I had to be as honest with

black students as I was with white students. My job was to present the culture honestly and passionately, realizing that only the student could choose what to take and what to reject from that culture. I had to assume an androgynous intellectualism; I had to be capable of holding two opposite points of view in my head at the same time and of offering each of them with conviction. I had to be honest, which meant that I had to rid myself of that inevitable white guilt about blacks and even risk being accused of cultural colonialism. But if that term still meant anything in the colleges, it was rapidly undergoing a metamorphosis: for it now signified the way in which the ghetto student had been intellectually patronized. His skin, rather than his intellect, was the only reality he was permitted. The teacher would reject the culture for him rather than ask him to define his needs in relation to that culture. In the process, he still had to grapple with ideas. A student, a Vietnam veteran in the program, once described an assignment in a speech class to me, a class designed to enable him to address the world in "purer" American. He had been asked to speak on what his teacher called a controversial subject. He chose to address himself to the causes of the war in Vietnam.

"When I'm finished," he said to me, "I can see her staring at me like I've done something wrong. Then she says, 'What about the black soldier in Vietnam?' And I knew she hadn't been listening to one word I'd said. I just looked at her and I didn't know what to do. I swear to you, I would have thrown up this whole college business then and there if I had followed my instincts. All she knew was that I was black and that there's a war on in Vietnam. Put two and two together and I've got to speak

on the black soldier. It's such crap. I read four books before I made that speech. I went to the library and I went
through I don't know how many articles. For the first
time in my life, I can understand why maybe this country
is going to hell. I lived in that library for a week and I
got to like it. I'm learning something about power, about
international politics. And all she can say to me when I've
finished is 'What about the black soldier?' You hear
that, you don't know what the hell to do. I'm not a
student to a teacher like that. I'm a *black* student. 'What
about the black soldier?' Jesus Christ."

It was not my place to enter into the conflict between
aspiration and background that confronted so many
students from the black ghetto. It took an exceptional
student to hold on to his militancy and his racial identity
while meeting the demands of an educational system
that he viewed with suspicion and distrust—and yet with
envy because he wanted the things it afforded. I had to
fight my own paternalism, my desire to interfere with
the lives of these students out of a superficial sense of
identification. Whether the student wanted to cut the
umbilical cord or drop out of the world of "Whitey's
culture" was his own business. I was not going to make
the task any easier for him. When all was said and done, I
was a product of that culture. And I believed in it.

In certain respects, my coming to terms with that
belief made the semester as successful as it was. Once
my students began to express themselves and I was faced
with the problem of helping them to avoid abstractions
in their thinking and writing, I discovered a renewed
vitalism in the very literary tradition I had begun to
doubt. It *was* a singular heritage. Shakespeare, Melville,
Milton became mine once again; their legitimacy could

be challenged and emerge renewed. "Kings as clowns is codgers—who ain't a nobody?" Melville had asked. I understood the question better now. Its message seemed implicit in teaching at City. The wall of academic standards had certainly not fallen, but a chink had at least been gouged out of it. And that was good. The books that had meant a great deal to me seemed to stand the test very well. That, too, was good.

The following semester I taught the second half of freshman English to another S.E.E.K. class of fourteen students. Our reading list included Camus' *The Stranger*, James's *The Beast in the Jungle*, Conrad's *Heart of Darkness*, Gide's *Pastoral Symphony*, Mann's *Mario and the Magician*, and Tolstoy's *The Death of Ivan Ilyich*. As we worked on these novels, I once again was reminded that teaching was an exciting profession, for I could see the movement toward awareness taking place. It was a different teaching experience only insofar as it forced me back into the validity of my own cultural tradition. The first remarks about *The Stranger* came from a student who had spent some time in jail, and he made the figure of Merseult even more real, even more isolated than he would otherwise have been. And the students went on from there, picking and choosing as I had done as an undergraduate: Camus, Sartre, Fanon. From Conrad they derived a picture of the conflict between Western and non-Western man; from Tolstoy they watched the final reality before which all men cringe; from Mann, the microcosm of politics in our century; from Gide, the lyric possibilities of tragedy. It was as relevant to their lives as it was to the lives of white students. It was only when I tried to project something I knew relatively little about and I pretended that their world was my own that the class moved away from me. They knew Langston Hughes's poetic portraits of Harlem from personal experience, but I was wrong to assume that his writing would capture them in a way that Yeats would not. They had to make the choices, both aesthetic and intellectual. I could not toy with them. And why should I have pretended to own something I did not? Why should I have assumed what reality was for them? As a freshman, I had enjoyed Michael Gold's *Jews Without Money*, a map of the territory out of which all city Jews sprang. When someone gave me a copy of Joyce's *Portrait of the Artist*, however, I had little difficulty in recognizing the truer frame for reality. Gold had written a memorable book; Joyce had written a great work of art that encompassed the coming-of-age experience and made it both total and absolute. His Dublin was even more real to me than Gold's Lower East Side, just as Yeats's dread in "The Second Coming" proved more accessible to many of these students than Langston Hughes's raisin suppurating in the sun. I had to learn—and it was a lesson that always demanded relearning—to leave students alone. City College was not intended to make black students comfortable any more than · had been intended to make white students comfortable.

I thought a great deal about my relationships with my students in 1967–68. I found that teaching had become a confusing profession. Difficult as the work was, the rewards of teaching in the S.E.E.K. program were fairly obvious. The students were intent on accomplishing something, and they helped provide their teachers with a sense of purpose. It was that very sense that was absent

183

in my other classes. By 1967 almost all the bright students in the college seemed afflicted in one way or another with a sense of purposelessness. Minds that had ranged freely, that had been critical and alive, now seemed sluggish and torpid. Students in the S.E.E.K. program had to be guided into the water and then permitted to swim on their own, while my students in the English honors seminar had been swimming in that water for so long they were beginning to wonder why they should keep it up. Had their dissatisfaction been with literature or with the intellectual life, I think I might have been able to help them. Unfortunately, theirs was a dissatisfaction with life in general, and it had seized an entire generation of college students. In spite of the talk about "dropping out," I sensed that these students were more interested in power than any other generation of students in the nation's history. Education did not really lead to power, at least not as these men and women understood it. And because it did not lead to power, it would have been futile to suggest that it might lead to a more meaningful knowledge. Students were not bored with Anglo-Saxon poetry, nor were they bored with Melville. They were bored with being.

Why were the rewards of teaching so much less in that honors class than in the S.E.E.K. class? Certainly not because I saw myself as a social crusader. The malaise that had enveloped my best students puzzled me. It was comparatively easy to combat ignorance and highly pleasurable to confront artificial sophistication. Indifference was something else. Ambition had died in these students, men and women both. How could I tell them why they were working so hard in their classes? Do you justify the study of literature? Do you pretend that its study will humanize the world, or do you discuss the power of imagination as beneficial to mankind? All of that was simply not true. Ultimately, the study of any discipline was self-serving.

My students were not looking for the kind of purpose that is distinctly political or even for advice on how to live their lives. What they wanted, strangely enough, was a missionary in the wilderness, a figure who would fill them with reverence and dread. I felt my own energies at a distance now. I did not want to convert anyone. Nor did I want to entertain. I could not give them what I thought they needed: a clear idea of the centrality of literature to their lives or even, if you will, a reason why their studies might offer alternatives to the pettiness around them. They were consumed with the questions of life styles, with the unspontaneous worship of the new and spontaneous, with the breakdown of intellectual and personal discipline, with the difficult thought that the mind, as much as the body, demanded expression.

The student malaise manifested itself in a kind of spiritual as well as intellectual disintegration. The press and television were soon filled with discussions of the American student, who was portrayed alternately as politically paranoid or withdrawn and uncaring. A similar disintegration was occurring among many American teachers, however. We were losing faith in the importance of what we were doing. I felt that I had to apologize for teaching literature when Vietnam, the growing black-white conflict, and student protest seemed so much more real. As my students handed in late paper after late paper, as I saw them stirred by an overwhelming desire for action in which cause and ego were momentarily blended, I found myself doubting the meaning of teaching in such times. The college passed from one crisis to another: Dow Chemical recruitment, the question of handing class standing over to selective service boards, the growing controversy over R.O.T.C., the attempt to make the administration more responsible to students and faculty alike. Many students began the retreat to privatism. Yet they were not the only ones who had lost faith in education. So many of my colleagues, like me, were suddenly questioning what they were doing. And they sounded despairing, their bewilderment changing day by day into lethargy, their activism giving way to pessimism.

There seemed to be no way out. I watched my brightest students turn apathetic, their intelligence consumed not by City or even by their educations but by the complex reality of being young in America. And the faculty suffered equally. None of us spoke about it very much, except to indicate how tired we, too, had become.

I was looking forward to my sabbatical the following year not because I wanted to return to Europe or even to write, although these were useful rationalizations, but really because I wanted time to think about what I was doing at City and why I was doing it. I felt disturbed by a need to justify myself and my profession. I was even more disturbed by the fact that I had, quite without knowing it, become a political creature. Teaching was now secondary in my own mind to the need to democratize the university. Once the ideal educational system came into being, I told myself, teaching would regain the importance it had been given in years past. A simple reality to admit. And it frightened me. For I suspected that I was using the need to change the universities in this country as an excuse to avoid coming to terms with the demands made on me as a teacher. I was behaving very much like the men I had dismissed as narrow academicians, who force the range and multiplicity of intellect into one or another niche and then build their careers around a single *idée fixe*. What they might do in the name of Marx or Freud or even the New Criticism, I was doing in the name of the students and their revolution. In my own mind, the students had by now become so completely central that virtually everything else was excluded. There was no room for scholarship, for criticism; there was no room for the kind of intellectual exploration that was exactly what I had to give to my students. I had begun to look upon students as martyrs to the cause of the democratic university, despite my uncomfortable feeling that they were simply impatient with language, with intellect, with the demands of education itself. Undergraduate education at City and throughout the country was becoming the victim of the uncertainty it had bred.

As my second three-year stint at the college came to an end, I felt as if my ego had been frayed down to its core. I felt as if a battle line had been drawn around the classroom and the act of teaching. And I was haunted by the idea that education itself had become an American no-man's-land. Forces were matched against one another. And I was left to wonder whether City could still maintain its function as a college and live up to its potential. Could it yet be made to speak for *all* of those who needed it, or would it simply be swallowed up in the conflict that threatened to consume America?

Chapter Seven

I spent my second Fulbright year in the Netherlands marking time. It was a fairly pleasant year, but as the months passed, I became more and more impatient to return to New York and to City College. Not that either New York or City were particularly attractive, even at a distance. Yet it was difficult to be a spectator to the anguish I had felt personally. That realization came to me one hot afternoon in late August, when I turned on a television set in an Amsterdam hotel only to see a friend at the Democratic convention being clubbed by Chicago police.

I felt no sense of involvement teaching at the University of Groningen. I was far more interested in the letters I received from New York, letters filled with despair about the state of the college, of the city, of the country. I was fortunate to be away, the writers all insisted. The teachers' strike in New York, the growing animosity between blacks and whites, the fiasco of the Democratic convention, the destruction of the promise that had been Czechoslovakia—all merged, threatening imminent apocalypse.

Some letters were vitriolic, others hysterical. Men who had prided themselves on a dispassionate sense of justice now demanded retribution. Intimations, rumors, threats and counterthreats, plots and counterplots. It was like viewing a movie where the reels were being shown at random. The college, meanwhile, reflected the insanity of the city. Distrust, animosity, group paranoias raging against each other.

City haunted me, as if being across the ocean bound me even closer to its fate. I used to go down once a week to the American embassy in the center of The Hague to search *The New York Times* for news items about the college. In my apartment I reread my colleagues' letters, which placed all the issues before me. The students, they said, were mixing cause with effect, tying one cause to another as they paraded their sexual "freedom" while shielding a Vietnam deserter in Finley Student Center; the college administration was agonizing in public, issuing one rhetorical statement after another; and the writer and his fellow members on the faculty were also to blame; not knowing which way to turn, they offered themselves first to the militant students, then to the administration. Animosities festered and finally, in April, the campus exploded.

I saw Finley Student Center burn on a Dutch television newscast. If it was difficult to piece together the incidents from the reports in the *Times* and from the hysterical letters, it was even more difficult to find out what had actually occurred when I returned in September. Few people could speak calmly about "the events of last spring." As far as I could tell, however, black militancy on campus had passed into the hands of the S.E.E.K. students, a change from the year before when these students had been essentially apolitical. They had apparently grown tired of the annual threats to the program that came from state and municipal politicians. Early in the spring semester, a group of S.E.E.K. students and their supporters issued a list of demands, which included a separate freshman orientation program, a student voice in the operation of S.E.E.K., a third world school with courses in black and Puerto Rican studies, and the immediate adoption of an open admissions policy. (The municipal college system had already pledged itself to admit all New York City high school graduates to some branch of the City University, but this program was not to begin until 1975.) When the demands were not met, a number of black and Puerto Rican students seized the south campus, renamed it the University of Harlem, and barricaded themselves within the gates. Afraid of open racial warfare, the college administration closed the entire campus for two weeks. Meanwhile, incidents multiplied. The faculty held daily meetings in which it criticized its own members as well as the students and the administration; the president of the college resigned; and one of the auditoriums in Finley Student Center was set on fire, reportedly by an "outsider." The University of Harlem soon faded into memory as several conditions set by the students, among them the demand for open admissions, were accepted by the board of higher education. The new policy was scheduled to begin in September, 1970. City's future had arrived.

I had been home for a week before I could bring myself to drive up to the college. The headlines in one of City's newspapers on my first day back vividly brought the college to life for me. "Badillo Declines Bid to Head the College"; "Urban, Ethnic Studies Dept. Created"; "College Plans for Additional Facilities and Adoption of 3-Semester Year to Implement 'Open Admissions' Plan"; "Board Sets Guidelines on Campus Disruptions." Article after article sounded the themes of the year to come. There was one story about a symposium on the future of the American university sponsored by *Playboy* magazine; another about the possibility of stripping R.O.T.C. of its credit; an article in which the acting president of the college was quoted as having told the United States Senate Permanent Investigations Subcommittee that student groups such as the Students for a Democratic Society and the DuBois Club were "treasonous and anti-American." Interspersed were stories about open admissions and its prospects for success, the drug problem on campus, the growing crime rate in the snack bar. All these articles implied that the college was on the verge of disintegrating. I closed the paper and walked over to the south campus cafeteria. New graffiti saluted me from the walls: "Big Pig Is Watching As We Get High." Underneath, a scribbled picture of an ugly porcine face.

I met a colleague and we began to talk. "It got to be like a Greek tragedy," he said, as we strolled around Finley. "You didn't know when it was going to end, or how. But there was a certain inevitability about it. You listened to speeches by the faculty and the students, and you kept on thinking that there was something, some primeval force, pulling the strings like a puppeteer.

"I suppose there's no way to make sense out of what happened. It was just crazy. There's nothing anyone can say either to justify it or to condemn it. It was just something that had to happen. At least that's what we started to tell ourselves after it was all over. I remember listening to all the speeches in Great Hall. After a while it got so that you couldn't identify the speaker or even which side he was on. I kept thinking that I had gone into this profession because I wanted a place where I could define myself. I wanted to get away from all the bullshit of politics and government and having to turn yourself into some goddamn mannequin. I never wanted to get caged by it, to become an ivory-tower academic. Well, now I find that mythical tower very attractive. The trouble with this college, the trouble with every college in this country, is that we really *are* at the center. All those slogans about the colleges being the future of America, the poor bastards don't know how right they are."

It was true. We were at the center of American consciousness. Our fantasies had finally caught up with us. We had taken on so much of the country's confusion, so many of its hostilities and ambitions, that we had become our own image of America. We professors now saw the role of a college in terms of our own public performance. The boarded-up windows of the burned-out auditorium testified to our confusion. Five years ago, when I had left for my first year abroad, it had been the streets of Harlem that had burned; this time, it had been the college. City had been rubbed down to its raw nerves, a symbol of New York and the country. What else could speak so nakedly about the state of siege that now afflicted urban man?

"I wish to hell they were wrong," sighed my friend.

"Who?"

"Those people who insist we remain at the center. I know it's necessary. I just wish there were some way we could keep the college separate from the nation." He waved at the boarded-up windows. "This school needs another championship basketball team."

"It could use another Aronow Auditorium, too." The last time I had been in Aronow, I remembered, had been for an antiwar poetry reading.

"Maybe," he said. "But it needs a basketball team more."

I don't know what I expected when classes began the following week. Perhaps I wanted to discover that the college had miraculously come to terms with itself, that the events of the previous spring had purged it of all its destructive impulses. Now that I was back, though, the first thing I had to do was to redefine my own feelings about City College.

And what exactly were they? More than ever before, the college seemed a microcosm of New York, of all big cities in this country. The tension on the campus was the tension of the streets transposed to an academic setting. I hungered for the dream of working-class excellence that had once given teaching here a peculiar glamour. I still longed for that lost country of the imagination. Perhaps it was simply because City had served New York well in the past. That much, at least, could truthfully be said of it, and I did not really want to separate the reality of the college from that past.

City's spring explosion had crystallized several problems. We teachers were going to have to redefine our function in terms of the kind of college we wanted and the kind of society that college reflected. Above all, we had to ask ourselves what prices had to be paid and who had to pay them. During my first few weeks back, I spoke to many people with whom I had worked in the antiwar movement and in the faculty movement whose goal was to redistribute City's administrative power. The faculty left was divided and disheartened, maintaining different points of view seemingly irreconcilable. Some dismissed all questions of class and maintained that skin color was the only crucial factor to the harmonious university; others insisted that the college remain dedicated to the quest for academic excellence. In some respects, political Left and Right fused; the new standard was opportunism. Men who in the past had passionately advocated the elitist university now argued for change, with one eye on Gracie Mansion and the other on "relevant" education. They were crippled by insecurities and by a lack of real intellectual perceptions about the college's situation. Occasionally a colleague might hint that blacks were not really capable of abstract reasoning. Had they *earned* the intellectual equality that they demanded? The cash-and-carry of American education: *earning*.

By the time classes began, no one could speak about life at the college with great enthusiasm. Voices were muted and sober. The only hope of both students and faculty that September was that we might get through the year. After a week, no one feared a repetition of "the events of last spring," yet few people ventured opinions on the future of the college.

A major difference that fall was the number of black faces on campus. Maybe it was just that blacks were now more visible at City; black group consciousness and solidarity had actually been growing since the mid-sixties. In what way, I began to wonder, would the larger black and Puerto Rican populations of the college affect my feelings about the white students at City, with whom I shared a strong sense of ethnic and class identification. City was changing from a college whose student body was predominantly Jewish to one basically composed of blacks and Puerto Ricans and white ethnic groups. Intellectually or even politically I could see that this change was necessary, but I could not tell how I would personally respond to it.

City had bred a New York provincialism in me, which heightened my perspective on American life while it distorted that life by narrowing the spectrum. During the first half of the decade, students had been excited by ideas and books. Intellectually combative, talmudists unaware of the existence of the Talmud, they lingered after class or in my office to challenge ideas and exchange views. They gloried in language, believed in the necessity of European high culture and the reality of Heming-way's myth of the American man. They respected their teachers more than their teachers deserved. They still believed, as generations of City students before them had believed, in the necessity of excellence.

History had rendered them unfashionable, and they were being punished for it. The new social critics were now asking whether they deserved to be saved. It occurred to me that these students had few alternatives to City. Elementary economic realities had been theirs by right of birth. A few of my colleagues had recently adopted a new concept of social responsibility, however, and the economics of the situation really didn't make too much difference to them. Open admissions, they said, would bring to City College the white student who had formerly gone to St. Francis or to L.I.U. This somehow made the program less worthwhile, less meaningful. Once again, white students were lumped together under the middle class banner, this time by the liberals and intellectuals.

While it angered me, it also put me on the defensive in a situation already clouded by rhetoric. Everyone was choosing sides. It seemed ludicrous to me that society's debt to blacks was now supposed to be paid by the Jews and the Italians and the Irish and the Greeks; I could not see why alleviating the greater misery should eradicate the lesser ones. My radical colleagues agreed with me, but some had great reservations. The oppression that white city dwellers endured had become essentially invisible to the suburbanite professors, even those who had attended City College as undergraduates. Strangely enough, they had a better idea of what life was like in Harlem than of what it was like in Washington Heights. They passed through Harlem on the way to the college every day; they lived during a period in history when black solidarity appeared effective and enviable, and they were attracted to the idea of black revolutionaries remaking America, leaving the world fresh and clean and new. At times they dismissed themselves as obsolete; at other times they viewed themselves as the intellectual foundation of the coming apocalypse. Their attitude toward blacks, a mixture of admiration and paternalism, inevitably complicated their attitudes toward white students at the college. They no longer denied reality by insisting on black inferiority; instead, they distorted it by demanding black superiority.

I felt I now had to make the attempt not to group white students together but to see them as individuals. If I were to maintain self-respect as a teacher and an intellectual, I had to be critical of all spontaneity and mindlessness, all desires to categorize and label. What did the term *middle class* mean to those who used it so loosely? Which of us finally was going to see himself as a spokesman for the children of the middle class plumber and his wife living in a rent-controlled apartment on Pelham Parkway? For that family on Pelham Parkway did not, after all, fit into our acceptable vision of status and obligations. They did not read *The New York Review of Books* or even the *Times*; they did not understand the values of the "new consciousness." They were highly intolerant of ideas—we professors somehow knew this without having bothered to speak to them— just as they were highly intolerant of long hair, of peaceniks, the new Catholicism, group sex, and LSD. They were targets for ridicule, even for their own children.

The faculty Left no longer accepted the reality of class, the very reality with which they should have been most sympathetic. About six weeks after the fall semester began, I met a friend of mine in the history department who had been involved in the antiwar movement at the college. When I asked him how he had fared the previous spring, he shrugged. "Well, it didn't make me into a conservative, if that's what you're asking. It did make me question some things though."

"Such as."

"I suppose I was facing the problem that we're all going to face in the future. I was sympathetic to the mood of the black students and to a great deal of what they were saying. But there's this terrible problem that

no one wants to talk about. You cut beneath the rhetoric
and what do you find? Class is color and color is class.
I think that's too limited, too simple. When you hear
people who think of themselves as radical endorsing it,
even if they're endorsing it through their silence, then
you begin to wonder whether what we're doing isn't
just reinforcing an illusion simply because it's convenient at the moment." He paused. "You know, we
have a faculty who accept things in toto or not at all.
There were nights last spring when the whole thing
seemed a naïve game, like color war in summer camp.
Here were all these people talking about the future
of the college, and yet nobody was really trying to look
at what this college should be. Who are we serving
here?"

Neither of us could feel comfortable in a situation
in which radicalism was so distorted. In the college, as
in the nation, the new Puritanism was rampant. Guilt
was widespread and indiscriminate. Allegiances were
being demanded of us. How far were we willing to go
in our pursuit of the proper radicalism? Especially in a
time when radicalism itself had been largely divested
of substance and had become a fad. The radical atmosphere on the campus was mistrustful and suspicious.
The moralistic quest for virtue that pervaded proved
unable to create a political reality. No longer was there
a faculty Left at the college, not, at least, one that
applied intellectual analysis to our situation.

At the college, experiment became its own justification, for the future was uncertain. Teaching had de-
generated into a relentless pursuit of vindication. But
the intellectual structure itself was reduced to an amorphous state. The curriculum no longer retained any

198

structure, having been "liberated" the previous year, and was able to promise everything because it did not have to deliver anything at all. No one on the faculty saw himself as primarily an intellectual. Developing one's intellect took second place to the task of restoring one's ego.

We teachers, who should have known better, adopted our students' belief that the only way to work through intellectual confusion was to define ourselves politically. The very real issues of the political situation—Vietnam, Cambodia, the continuing racial crisis—made this an important part of self-definition. In our demand for apocalypse, we sought to escape from these issues through politics. Politics had become religion. During the winter of 1969–70, I was aware that most of us were no longer sure of what we stood for or of what we could achieve. So many of my colleagues—in history, in physics, in English—had lost faith in the "relevance" of their disciplines, as if intellectualism had to provide immediate rewards or not exist at all. If students weren't interested in physics anymore, then the fault lay not with the students nor with the teachers but with the discipline. A way had to be found that would make physics more immediate, less difficult, and, inevitably, more "relevant." Education was no longer an extension of adult society but an in-between world, a last chance to share in a belated adolescence. We had become collective creatures forged together by the national mood. We wanted not to educate our students but to be loved by them. We professors, too, had taken up the burden of the country, with its sense of purposeless brutality. We, too, could turn ourselves into monosyllabic creatures of the faith; we abandoned our former distance, our cloak of language and intellect, for the opportunity to be close to our students. In the past, language had been a means *toward* self-expression. Now we were even willing to abandon language in our need to be kindred to the student.

Our abdication was evident in the restructuring of the curriculum. We competed with our students to make a City College education more "relevant." Undoubtedly the curriculum revision was long overdue, and yet there was something self-serving in our approach to it. During my year abroad, I had developed a course entitled "The Political Novel," my addition to the large number of new courses listed in the college bulletin. "Literature and Society," "The Legend of Odysseus," "The Hero in American Literature," "The Literature of Mysticism," "Mythic Patterns in Modern Literature," along with four courses on black literature, were some of the English department's new offerings.

The curriculum changes were too facile to be meaningful. We viewed the past as an intellectual potpourri from which we extracted books and ideas at random. No demand, no slogan, no half-formed idea was too farfetched, yet all discussions dissipated into political posturing. What Lukács had written of Mann brought forth a stifled yawn; the class became animated only when the room echoed with the latest pronouncements of Jerry Rubin or the revolutionary word of Eldridge Cleaver. Why read *Dr. Faustus* when *Slaughterhouse Five* was so much more relevant? "Fascism is not *our* problem, Dr. Kriegel." Why not examine *Naked Lunch* as the ultimate literary act of political protest in America? Words were words. "The Political Novel" course failed both me and my students, for we had reached the point at which ideology and art were pitted against one another. Any claims to substance were soon destroyed as the actors, teacher and students, took their places onstage. Like my students, I was more than willing to move away from the flesh and pain of the novel, which threatened me as much as it did them with the complexities of humanity. Ideologies alone would suffice, no matter how superficial and distorted the politics. Adolescent voices insisting on Auden's "necessary murder"—the students claimed their ideologies.

It was a time of reckoning in the academic world. Each teacher was trying to balance out his life. America had not lived up to our expectations, yet it seemed important, as never before, to continue teaching. If it were no longer possible to define oneself through the profession, it might yet prove possible to redefine why teaching was important. However weary we might be, the college still survived. By the fall 1970 semester, City College had weathered animosities and tensions for so long that it was used to them, accepted them as it did the "temporary structures" where I still taught my classes and where I would probably be teaching my classes years from now. The faculty had pulled up short, preparing itself for another holding action that might reveal how it could make itself useful again.

As a teacher, as an intellectual, as a member of the college faculty, I felt totally split by contradictions but tended to make decisions based on old values. Although I believed in the necessity of new modes of education and experimentation in the classroom, I nonetheless found myself placing greater and greater reliance on the traditional cultural orientation to which I had been exposed as an undergraduate. It now had greater meaning for me. I thought of myself as egalitarian, but I wanted to avoid the kind of faculty-student relationships that now patronized professors as the professors had once patronized students. I insisted on the educational rights of blacks, but I wanted to be assured that the cost of their long-overdue equality would not be borne by those white students who needed "free" education and City College as much as the blacks did.

By late 1970, I felt less capable of judging my peers. I could only observe them, for their actions were as confused as my own. The problems of this college faculty could be found on almost any college campus in the country. At New Haven, at Berkeley, at Cambridge, there were other men and women who had decided to become teachers and scholars. Not, certainly, a momentous decision, as the world measures such things. A profession, a way of working through, of existing in this world. They had not initially viewed college teaching as a form of self-abnegation, but somewhere along the line they had put themselves in the background in order to fulfill a new function. A teacher was now required to fight for causes, to be ready and willing to do combat of all kinds—with the public, with the administration, with his fellow faculty, with the students, with everybody and everything except his intellect. We now discovered that we were caught between constituencies, trapped between our loyalty to our students and the demands of our training. We had come to the point where we were willing to consider any solution to America's educational ills, no matter how unrealistic it might sound; it was time now to take a step backward. Our indecisiveness had affected our students, too. Students at City in 1970 were among the most rigid and self-doubting young people I had ever confronted. They saw themselves as strangers in their own land. They were losing faith in the traditional culture, and they were asking their teachers to make their choices for them. By now, though, there had been too many claims upon our allegiance. It was time to turn our attention to the critical question facing us: just what was a college education intended to do for the student? It was time to be realistic about our limitations, to scale down our conception of academia and reassess our expectations of it with full awareness that our responsibilities, both intellectual and social, were the responsibilities of democratic education.

At City, chief among those responsibilities was ensuring the success of open admissions. It was imperative that the new policy succeed, both for itself and as a flexible model for what might be achieved in the nation. What we were moving toward was an idea of higher education as a right rather than as a prerogative granted either by wealth or by social acceptability. It was this that made open admissions so promising as a concept and so susceptible to failure.

When open admissions began in the fall of 1970, there was little talk about its problems and prospects, only a great deal of faculty and student grumbling about the incredibly crowded conditions. Simply moving from place to place on campus had become a formidable challenge. The planning of the board of higher education had not accounted for the physical demands such a program would present the college. I suspect that the planning reflected a basic lack of enthusiasm for the open admissions program and that the bureaucratic hierarchy of the board of higher education was really interested in more important matters, such as the flourishing Graduate Center at Forty-second Street. Never had an academic program been asked to do so much, having been given so little to do it with. Students complained about the difficulties of finding a place to eat, about the indignities of crowded washrooms, about the physical energy required simply to maneuver through the densely packed corridors. City had never been a school at which students or faculty expected the physical amenities that are taken for granted elsewhere. But the school now resembled a subway rush hour that lasted from 9 A.M. until 4 P.M. Teachers battled to get to classes on time, to squeeze into half a parking space, to claim a desk in an office— their own or anybody else's—in order to prepare lectures or grade papers or speak to a student about his work in private.

And yet, from its inception, open admissions offered City a new educational mission that might allow it to survive. The problems posed by the program sometimes appeared so overwhelming as to be insoluble. As I write this, in December of 1971, there is no indication that the problems have been successfully resolved. The City College was simply going to be a different institution from what it had been in the past, and we were going to have to accept that fact. City had once been one of the best undergraduate institutions in the country, but now the college was suddenly populated by a student body unlike any other in its history. Our students of the late sixties had also been blacks and blue-collar whites, but by the fall 1971 semester, half of the entering freshman class needed some kind of remedial work in English. Queens and Brooklyn colleges were now attracting the kind of student who had attended City when I was teaching there in 1961. The day when City had been the academic jewel in the municipal college system's crown had ended. We had to face the prospects before us. They were fascinating but very different. Open admissions required the introduction of remedial programs on a massive scale, but I was absorbed with the opportunity to teach in the experimental humanities course. If this program was to succeed, then a new type of intellectual relationship between teacher and student would be needed. Open admissions was very exciting, and I felt this especially when I watched the students on campus and listened to my younger colleagues discussing their work in the remedial programs. Of course, I had to admit that the college was undergoing an intellectual metamorphosis. All American colleges were, but the phenomenon was more visible at City than elsewhere. Open admissions accentuated the changes by forcing us to confront a number of educational myths and realities.

As always at City, the students represented the fundamental reality. The freshmen somehow reminded me of the students I had taught a decade earlier at L.I.U. Those students had also been categorized by a society distrustful of their presence and suspicious of their ambitions; they, too, had been warned of their imminent failure for so long that they had come to accept it as fact. For many of them, reality had been determined by their own limitations. The complaints about them sounded familiar. "How do they do it at Harvard?" was still not so distant a memory. Interestingly enough, the complaints were not usually voiced against the large numbers of black students now entering the college. Racism, too, was in the throes of a reversal. Open admissions had admitted a significant number of white students who would not have been accepted at City in the past. These were the students who were soon labeled "dead" or "boring." "I offered to teach remedial work because I thought I was going to get a group of inarticulate but vibrant blacks. Instead, they give me a group of dumb Jews. I really resent that." Blacks were still expected to be inarticulate but revolutionary; teaching them allowed us to imagine ourselves at the center of history. Where, we asked ourselves, were the bright, intellectually aggressive students who had once been synonymous with City College? Were they deserting the college en masse? If so, where were they to be found? Maybe those students had fled the country; perhaps they were going underground.

It was interesting to observe the white and black students now at City. The blacks projected an attractive cohesiveness and group solidarity; the whites appeared confused and resentful. By the spring of 1971, more and more students were rallying around one or another ethnic banner. A new American proletariat might yet emerge from the children of blue-collar whites, and they might soon reject the ambitions their parents had for them. These students now demanded attention; they insisted on being viewed as individual men and women with individual problems. I wondered what would happen if their anger, which was usually turned inward and was essentially self-destructive, were ever to be politicized.

During the first semester of open admissions, debates about scholarship were renewed. In the past, the prospects for promotion had been the most discussed aspect of the scholarly life. Even those faculty members most sympathetic to open admissions searched for something else to make their profession more meaningful. We needed relief from academia's long years of dissension. The dangers now threatening our profession no longer came from militant students or angry taxpayers venting their frustrations against "those goddamned professors." We were in far greater trouble because of what we had done to ourselves. We needed the very values we had put away for the past few years: dispassionate thinking and intellectual endeavor. America's social chaos made the temptation to withdraw overwhelming, yet it seemed shameful not to be "committed." But to what, exactly, could we now commit ourselves? We were doomed to failure in either case, whether we viewed our students as the "new unwashed" or whether we constructed a fantasy of the new revolutionary man from them. Perhaps all we could successfully do was to enable them to see the validity of their own experience. My task, as I saw it, was to defend what was healthy and vital in the culture. Still, I had to permit the student freedom of choice, to let him take what he felt he needed and let go of what was not important to him.

The open admissions student seemed less volatile than his predecessors. The program had apparently brought a more tractable student body to the college. These were students who were not used to making demands or who believed that they did not have anything to demand. The campus grew quieter. Students either did not want to be bothered with politics, or else they wanted to return to traditional classroom situations; they were asking to be taught. In certain respects, it was somewhat depressing. Students had been quite vocal about the need for independence and equality, but when they were offered independence, they decided they would rather not accept the responsibility. They wanted more than guidance; they wanted direction. The revolution might yet come to America; the battlefield, however, was no longer going to be the classroom.

The new president of the college, who took office in September, 1970, wanted City to remain an institution of intellectual excellence, although he acknowledged the necessity of making significant social and economic changes. The goal was to educate those who in the past had been considered uneducable. He undoubtedly didn't know whether City could maintain a position of educational importance as it accepted the realities of open admissions. At least he had some idea of the problems that a public urban institution would have to face during the next decade. His chances for success, like those of the college, were real, even if they were not bright.

Few of us could now understand the roots of student passivity; several years earlier we had not been able to understand the reasons for student anger and unrest. It was too easy to blame everything on the times. However, more of us were now willing to struggle within the cultural framework and to speak out for what we believed rather than for what we thought our militant students wanted us to believe. Slowly we teachers were beginning to retreat from our indiscriminate guilt feelings. It now seemed possible to acknowledge the value of intellect and imagination as elements of individuality rather than as substitutes for them. To explain to students exactly how language performed its function again be-

208

came our working reality. We felt strong enough to
accept the challenge from our students and learn to
work with a variety of educational methodologies, ex-
tracting the best each had to offer. We could encourage
our students to explore for themselves, as so many of
us had been encouraged. First, however, we had to give
them something to struggle with.

Whatever its faults and no matter how uncertain its
future prospects, City College in December, 1971, was
a natural part of the world again. I felt a fresh enthusiasm for teaching because of what was happening
to my students. They seemed to be reading once again.
And learning now seemed important to them. Perhaps
this meant no more than a momentary respite from
chaos, or perhaps it represented the channeling of political weariness into traditional American pragmatism. All
I knew was that educating students was not only possible now, it was once again central to my own life. It
felt good to be a teacher. It hadn't felt as good for a long
time.

I remain skeptical. The dimensions of change in the
academic world have expanded so rapidly that a wary
skepticism is almost demanded as a form of self-protec-
tion. After all, there is a fifty-fifty chance that the
critics of open admissions may prove to be correct in
their prophecies; the program may yet bring the college
down. Public funds are drying up; the nation is in
trouble; the city is in even greater trouble. The cry of
"No money!" is a familiar one. The democratic experiment in higher education may yet succumb to the dilemmas of urban man in America. If so, the fate of City

College may foretell the ultimate fate of all urban university centers.

Despite my doubts and the evidence supplied by its critics, I prefer to believe that open admissions may still lead us in a different and more promising direction. It seems to me that we are just beginning to live up to Townsend Harris' idea of opening the educational doors to all. City College may truly be Mr. Harris' revenge upon New York. Can we turn the college into an urban model for the nation? Fragmentary evidence indicates that there are still avenues open to urban man. Above all, there are the students. At City we have never really had very much to work with except our students. Somehow they have always proved to be enough.